# SUBJECT CATALOGUES
## HEADINGS AND STRUCTURE

# SUBJECT CATALOGUES

## HEADINGS AND STRUCTURE

By

E. J. COATES

LA

THE LIBRARY ASSOCIATION

LONDON

Published by
Library Association Publishing Ltd
7 Ridgmount Street
London WC1E 7AE

First published 1960
Reprinted 1969
Reissued with new preface 1988

ISBN 0-85365-678-9

Printed and made in Great Britain by Redwood Burn Ltd, Trowbridge, Wilts.

# CONTENTS

# PREFACE TO FIRST EDITION

In 1955 the Publications Committee of the Library Association approached my chief, Mr. A. J. Wells, with a request that he should write a book on subject cataloguing. At the time, Mr. Wells was preoccupied with the inauguration of the British National Bibliography Card Service, and he made the suggestion, which was agreed by the Committee, that I should undertake the task. The result is scarcely an adequate substitute for the book which Mr. Wells would have written. Nevertheless, he has had a major part in shaping my views on subject cataloguing, and in this sense the present book stems back to him, though he might not subscribe to all the views now put forward.

I am also especially indebted to two groups of people, with whom I have had the opportunity to discuss and argue many of the issues dealt with here. These are, first, the colleagues who have shared with me the rigours of subject cataloguing for the *British National Bibliography*. Their contribution has been much greater than they know. Secondly, many of the ideas which I have tried to elaborate, had their origin or gained clarification in discussions with fellow-members of the Classification Research Group.

I am grateful to Mr. Wells, to Mr. D. G. Foskett, to Mr. B. C. Vickery, and to Mr. B. I. Palmer for reading the text, offering valuable suggestions, and generally saving the book from the worst pitfalls. Mr. Palmer also took it upon himself to prod, spur, and encourage, whenever he sensed that the work was flagging. Had he not proved irresistible, the book might never have been completed. He finally rounded off his most valued assistance by helping to read the proofs.

I have to thank Mr. J. E. L. Farradane and Dr. S. R. Ranganathan for their help in clarifying a number of problems which arose in the course of writing chapters V and IX. My thanks are also due to Miss Beatrice Herzfeld for help in typing, and to Mr. F. J. Cornell, Publications Officer of the Library Association, for his efficient and considerate handling of the details of publication.

In connection with copyright requirements, acknowledgement is here made, as follows: to the Council of the British National Bibliography, for permission to reproduce numerous index entries and headings from the *British National Bibliography* and the *British Catalogue of Music*; to the Forest Press, Inc., New York, for permission to quote from the Introduction and Index to the 14th edition of the *Decimal classification*; to Messrs. H. W. Wilson, Inc., New York, for permission to print an extract from the Index to H. E. Bliss's *Bibliographical Classification*; and to Dr. S. R. Ranganathan for allowing me to quote from his *Classified Catalogue Code*.

Although the work has not been written with an eye to the Library Association Syllabus, it is hoped that it may be useful to students at Registration or Final level, who, having perhaps covered the groundwork in standard textbooks on cataloguing, may wish to take a closer look at some of the underlying issues in this sector of the field. It is also intended as a working aid to practising cataloguers.

E. J. COATES

British National Bibliography,
London, W.C.1.
*October* 1959.

# PREFACE TO 1988 REISSUE

## DATED, BUT NOT NECESSARILY OUTDATED

*Subject catalogues*, now being reissued 28 years after its original publication date, strongly reflects a point-of-view on subject indication for retrieval associated with a particular place and time, namely the United Kingdom around 1960. In this sense it is obviously a dated work. It is not too hard to find in the book terminological anachronisms which confirm this. For instance 'mechanical selector', though of impeccable pedigree to those familiar with the very beginning of the mechanisation of information stores, falls strangely on the ear in the late 1980s. Its use in 1960 reflects the then lingering misconception that computers were essentially huge and very fast calculators, and that some kind of variant but still computer-like hardware would be required for the storage of information for retrieval. Another apparent quirk of a terminological kind is the absence from the text of 'information language', 'indexing language' or 'documentation language', though the concept to which these phrases refer was in fact central to the ideas in the book. The fullness of time in which they were to enter the common currency of professional discourse had evidently, in the author's understanding, not yet arrived. However, despite these and other signs of antiquity, a reissue has been called for, suggesting perhaps that it does not follow that a dated work is also necessarily outdated. It is true that during the quarter-century in question very much water indeed, mostly associated with mechanisation of bibliographic records, has flowed under bridges, in connection with subject indication. The questions that the reissue after so long an interval provoke are what influence, if any, did the book have on subsequent developments in the field of subject indication, and if it had no immediate influence, is there any sense in which the developments have, after a meandering progress, turned full circle or nearly full circle in such a manner as to refocus attention on *Subject catalogues*.

## AIMS AND MOTIVATION

Firm answers to the above questions would more fittingly come from others than the author, and this preface to the reissue confines itself to some suggestions as to points which, no doubt among others not covered here, might need to be considered in coming to conclusions.

It is perhaps useful to begin with a brief explanation of the motivation for writing the book in the first place. That it was undertaken at all is due to the friendly and flattering persuasion of others, most notably A.J. Wells, the first Editor of the *British National Bibliography*. The original preface states that it was targetted both at advanced students and at practising subject cataloguers. Essentially the book had a two-fold purpose, comprising what may be called a down-to-earth element and a higher-flying element. The down-to-earth motive was a wish to present, for those familiar with the *B.N.B.* application of Ranganathan's principles, and with the publicly exposed product of this application, a discussion of these same principles in a more generalised context. As to how the *B.N.B.* came to be involved in such an exercise, this will shortly become clear below in considering the second, or higher-flying motive, which was to try to introduce into subject indication professional practice generally a greater element of systematic structure, procedural regularity and 'rulyness' than had been the norm before the appearance of *B.N.B.*.

## SUBJECT INDICATION AS AN INTUITIVE ART OR CRAFT

For the student or the practical decision-maker, seeking an underlying intellectual coherence which would give him predictive capability – the capability of making decisions which would later turn out to be in line with some standard practice of a central or co-ordinating agency – the mainstream of subject indication theory and practice in the English speaking world has been and remains something of a disappointment. As a largely intuitive craft, unable to formulate or communicate any clear-cut rationale explaining its procedures, it incorporates a quaking morass of largely unconnected ad hoc precepts and a dearth of comprehensive rules which might form the basis of a unifying discipline.

The U.S. Library of Congress National Union Catalogue and its predecessors, together with the associated list of Library of Congress subject headings were for many years up to about 1960 the standard-bearers for mainstream subject indication, and they were widely emulated as authoritative models. Their influence both within the U.S. and worldwide was formidably reinforced by the availability of the Library of Congress centralised card catalogue service, a unique facility in the manual era.

## GLIMPSES OF A POSSIBLE RATIONALE

*Subject catalogues* attempts a brief and selective survey of the mainstream subject indication intuitive craft, ranging over about eight decades preceding 1960. It devotes special attention to rare endeavours to propound cogent and comprehensive intellectual procedures for subject indication which occurred from time to time. These unusual events roused interest as they occurred, but any effect they had upon the craft-oriented mainstream was by and large shortlived. They are associated with such names as Cutter, Kaiser, Ranganathan and Farradane. These endeavours were variously incomplete or fragmentary, but taken together they seemed to point in an agreed direction. Of them all, those of Ranganathan were the most fully elaborated and the most durable in continuing to arouse interest. Nevertheless in the 1970s and 1980s vast numbers of new lexical tools for retrieval have been set up, for whose devisers Ranganathan might as well not have existed. Even well into the mechanised retrieval era, intuition-based subject indication has held its own.

## THE BRITISH NATIONAL BIBLIOGRAPHY– DEPARTURE FROM THE INTUITIVE MAIN STREAM

The *British National Bibliography* from its inception in 1950 until its incorporation into the British Library in 1970 marks a decisive break with the idea of subject indication as an intuitive craft. The classified form of catalogue had a slight predominance in U.K. libraries at this time over other forms. Accordingly the Bibliography was set up as a subject systematic file backed up by an alphabetical subject index for primary access. In connection with this decision, the question of possible compatibility with Library of Congress practice arose, only to be abandoned when it became apparent that the technical difficulties of reaching compatibility would be insurmountable. In the Library of Congress itself at that time classification and subject heading work were independent and organisationally unrelated activities. There was thus no possibility of any kind of mapping of the U.S. practice on to the British preferred file format. The practice was too ill-defined to make such a mapping possible. The *B.N.B.* accordingly adopted the far better defined Ranganathan system, which had however not previously been brought into operation outside Ranganathan's own Colon Classification. The *B.N.B.*'s terms of reference required it to use the Dewey Decimal Classification for the arrangement of its systematic file. The ideas set out in *Subject catalogues* were the product of a decade's experience in applying Ranganathan's principles to the classifying by D.D.C. of the British published output of monographs, under the extremely demanding deadlines required for current weekly publication of the *B.N.B.*

## SUBJECT INDICATION AS A UNITARY DISCIPLINE

The first step along the road of formulating a coherent set of working and fully communicable rules for subject indication was to try to establish subject indication as a unitary field embracing the hitherto separated spheres of classification and alphabetical subject indexing and cataloguing. On this there does seem to have been something of a sea change in professional opinion since 1960. In the 1980s the essential unity of these activities hitherto regarded as diverse is so widely recognised that the case no longer needs arguing. It seems reasonable to suppose that *Subject catalogues* may well have played some part in bringing this change about. The profession is still however less convinced by the proposition clearly implied in *Subject catalogues* that within this unified framework all information languages need to be based upon a classification system. The author's view on this remains unchanged, but there is a deep irony here in that his later activity in devising the *British Technology Index* indexing system without benefit of formal back-up by a single classification system, has been held by some, including Ranganathan himself, as showing that a classification system is not an indispensable basis for controlled alphabetical subject indication. The answer to this is that the *B.T.I.* system's formal independence from a classification system was a matter of necessity rather than of virtue. There was no suitable classification available; it would have been a better indexing system had there been such a classification, and in fact much informal recourse to portions of a variety of classification systems was regularly employed as a necessary but decidedly second best procedure. The correct view is surely that while syntactic control of such systems as *B.T.I.* and PRECIS requires merely a generalised facet or relational frame-work, foolproof semantic control requires an actual classification scheme.

## INTERACTION BETWEEN MECHANISATION AND SUBJECT INDICATION

A consideration relevant to the second and wider element in the motivation for writing *Subject catalogues* was the fact that in 1960 the tide of mechanisation of information stores was visibly approaching the U.K. Though the book was at great pains – at too great pains, hindsight now suggests, to insist that it was derived from experience of manual subject indication work, it was written with a wary, but not unwelcoming, eye on impending mechanisation. It was thought, perhaps somewhat naively, that the existence of a rationally oriented body of thought on subject indication might help to channel the mechanisation tide, when it arrived, into more useful directions than if it interacted only with an art of subject indication. The tide in fact caught up with the author about four years after the completion of

*Subject catalogues*, when the first exploratory step was taken which ultimately, yet another four years on, resulted in an operational computer system for *British Technology Index*.

In retrospect, it is clear that no fresh ideas on subject indication surfacing in the early 1960s had a realistic chance of making any direct or immediate impact on the pattern of the mechanisers' initial solutions or part-solutions in the field of subject retrieval, which had already begun to gel even before the expansion of American mechanisation expertise into other countries.

## NEW PERSPECTIVE ON THE ROLE OF INFORMATION LANGUAGES

A more pertinent question concerns the possible impact that mechanisation has had upon the ideas set out in *Subject catalogues* and other channels carrying the Ranganathian message at that time. On the whole, mechanisation has widened perspectives and shifted emphases, but not appreciably negated nor impugned the validity of the outlook of *Subject catalogues*. However, for an example of an assumption that cannot now be defended, reference may be made to the declaration of the Dorking International Conference of 1957, to the effect that faceted classification is the basis of all information retrieval. While *Subject catalogues* avoided endorsing the declaration, someone reading the book in the 1980s would justifiably infer that the author was arguing that information languages were the basis of all retrieval methods, and that classification was or should be the basis of information languages. Mechanisation has shown that the first part of the foregoing proposition is too sweeping. The very large information stores which mechanisation makes it possible to set up and search have shown very clearly that information languages are not necessarily the basis for *all* retrieval. On the contrary, the basis of all retrieval is matching of identical sets of character strings, but some information retrieval tasks require the additional use of lexical aids, such as classifications and thesauri, though again not necessarily as we were apt to assume in the manual era, for the purposes of assigning subject labels to documents or document surrogates, but equally or more essentially as aids to the user in formulating and modifying searches. User queries of the general form: 'I want *some* information on X' can be satisfied by simple clerical matching, that requires no supplementation by the introduction of an information language into the retrieval process, provided that the store being interrogated is a large one. Those queries requiring *all* material in the store on subject X are not likely to be satisfied by simple matching alone, unless the store is very small and the subject field embraced by the store a very narrow one. Where recognition of this last category of query is not accorded, we have so-called free text indexing using simple matching of query word with title or text word. Where such recognition is accorded we have a thesaurus or some other form of information language brought into the retrieval process. Currently online systems perform better in dealing with the first type of query, than with the second type. The reason for this is fairly obvious. A simple matching procedure is inherently less complex than one which is combined with a translation step involving an information language either at document input or query input or both. This would be true even if information languages were free of imperfections of structure and formal consistency. They are in fact, in varying degrees, imperfect. The proliferation of thesauri of all kinds which accompanied large scale mechanisation, suggests that at one level, and after some initial ignoring of the distinction between ideas and the terms by means of which ideas are communicated, a majority of the mechanising fraternity did take on board the need for retrieval purposes always to distinguish concepts from terms. However at another level, that of the construction of thesauri themselves, this principle has been more honoured in the breach than the observance. Despite their distinctive and characteristic format, thesauri are often in many respects reincarnations of the intuitive craft-based American subject heading lists of the manual era.

## SEMANTIC AND SYNTACTIC AXES

Another vitally important aspect of subject indication which mechanisation has fortuitously helped to clarify is the matter of semantic and syntactic axes in the design and application of information languages. This question, though highly relevant to Ranganathan's inventions does not seem to have been fully explored by Ranganathan himself. In *Subject catalogues* it is encountered only in a piecemeal and implicit manner in connection with 'compound subjects'. It was noticeably studied by Gardin in the early 1960s, who, following ideas propounded by Saussure in the linguistics field, pointed out that subject indication needed to take account of two different kinds of subject relations, paradigmatic and syntagmatic. Paradigmatic relations are *a priori* relations between concepts, in which the relation is implied in the meaning of the concepts. These include the hierarchical and collateral relationships familiarly manifested in classification systems, and in a more fragmentary fashion in thesauri. In discourse, other than discourse about the relationships themselves, they are implied rather than stated. They may alternatively be termed semantic relationships. Syntagmatic or syntactic relationships are on the contrary *a posteriori*, explicit in discourse and expressed by word juxtaposition in sentences, by inflections and by prepositions. In this scheme of things Ranganathan's facets, with the possible exception of the elusive Personality Facet, express exclusively syntactic relations. Both kinds of relationship need to have provision made in information languages and in search strategies. In classificatory and thesaural structures the two kinds of relationship exist independently. In the light of the Gardin dichotomy it becomes apparent that recent progress in subject indication theory and in mechanised subject indication has been very largely on the syntactic relationship side alone. The semantic relation side of Ranganathan's classification, of the *B.T.I.* system, and later of PRECIS has recourse to existing convention, which depends in turn on a large element of intuitive craft. Similarly in mechanised retrieval it is the syntactical relations which most readily lend themselves to handling in connection with inverted files, post-coordination and the structure of thesauri.

## MECHANISATION – SUBJECT INDICATION INTER-ACTIONS AT THE NON-TECHNICAL LEVEL

Questions such as those discussed above, such as the respective roles of free-text matching and use of information languages in retrieval, of the syntactic and semantic axes, and of the underlying common factors in all forms of subject indication, refer to areas in which there has been interaction between mechanisation techniques and subject indication techniques, at the level of ideas or of practice or of both. However subject indication has been more conspicuously affected by the political-economic and management entourage and culture associated with computers. In the present author's view many of these effects have been negative from the point of view of technical excellence and their economic justification open to doubt.

When one surveys the subject indication facilities offered by many of the great bibliographic databases and their hosts, when, nearer home, one considers the virtual demise from 1971 onwards of the *British National Bibliography* as a systematic conspectus for browsing and comprehensive broad search, the dropping of the *B.C.M.* classification from the *British Catalogue of Music*, the changes in format and arrangement in the former *British Technology Index* from 1981, and the reversion in some library school curricula to the old class/cat partitioning of subject indication as a field of study one might reasonably conclude that whatever influence *Subject catalogues* may have had on the theory of subject indication, its effect on large scale practice appears to have been merely transient.

However a swing of the pendulum, reflecting the generally high regard in which the book has been held, is by no means out of the question. Favourable and sometimes enthusiastic estimation of the book has outweighed damnation by faint praise and downright disapproval. The positive views seem to have survived many years of the out-of-print condition. Some of the negative views have usefully thrown sideways light on why a reissue is necessary. One of the most severe critics once explained to the author why he used *Subject catalogues* as a text for classroom teaching though its views were anathema to him. Apart from the opportunity it afforded him for shooting down what he did not like, he ruefully but generously declared that he did not know of another book which presented the essential features of subject indication in quite the same satisfactory way. By contrast, Ranganathan himself approved of the book, overlooking its occasional heresies, but added the admonition that one cannot teach by the printed word alone. Possibly these two comments taken together offer a hint as to both the limitations of *Subject catalogues* and the special niche which it seems to have acquired for itself within the body of more up-to-date and more widely ranging literature on subject indication.

E.J. Coates
November 1987

# CHAPTER I

# TERMINOLOGY

ANY discussion of subject cataloguing, as of other techniques at a comparable stage of development, is hampered by a lack of precise terminology. There are two ways of meeting this difficulty. The first is to invent new words and phrases with unequivocal meanings; in other words, to use a technical jargon. This is the ideal way of avoiding the ambiguity consequent upon the use of terms capable of various shades of meaning, but it has the very serious disadvantage of demanding positive mental efforts from the reader before his interest is engaged. The other method is to use old words or phrases with their respective ranges of meaning arbitrarily restricted or extended to suit the purpose of the argument. In this book a compromise is adopted, heavily biased to the second method. The notes which follow give an explanation of the sense in which some of the commoner key words and phrases are used.

CATALOGUE and INDEX are used interchangeably in the text. The generally accepted difference between them is that an index entry merely locates a subject, whereas a catalogue entry includes some descriptive specification of a document containing the subject. But the line is not in practice hard and fast. Some famous catalogues have been called indexes, and the term is frequently used to cover the subject catalogues of a special library. Indexing is also often used to mean analytical subject cataloguing of a document. Miss Pettee[1] has a special use for the word 'index' which she applies to a subject catalogue based on catchwords derived from book titles. As this book is confined to subject headings, and the catalogue structure derived therefrom, without consideration of the descriptive body of the catalogue entry, it seems legitimate to treat the two as synonyms.

DOCUMENT is used in the extended sense, meaning any form of graphic, acoustic or haptic record (book, periodical, clipping, manuscript, map, etc.).

ENQUIRER is the term denoting anyone who consults the subject catalogue. It includes library staff as well as clients.

SUBJECT CATALOGUE refers to any kind of record which directs an enquirer from subject-terms to the documents dealing with them. By extension it may for our purposes be made to embrace subject indexes to individual books where the reference is to a location within the book. As used here, it will normally also cover subject bibliographies. The subject catalogue may be alphabetical or systematic in arrangement.

ALPHABETICO-SPECIFIC SUBJECT CATALOGUE is a subject catalogue in which the alphabetically arranged headings state precisely the subject of each document, chapter, section, paragraph, or other literary unit chosen as the basis for indexing. The subject part of a dictionary catalogue constructed on the specific entry principle is included in this definition.

ALPHABETICO-CLASSED SUBJECT CATALOGUE is an alphabetical subject catalogue, in which the entry words of the heading consist of selected generic subjects. Under each generic entry word, its included specific topics are cited as subheadings, and subarranged alphabetically. The stepping down process for citing more restricted subjects may be carried to further stages.

CLASSIFIED CATALOGUE is a subject catalogue in which the entries are arranged in systematic order, exhibiting hierarchical relationship between subjects, and some kind of helpful order (order of complexity, chronological order, pedagogical order, or occasionally alphabetical order) between co-ordinate subjects on the same hierarchical level. The two parts of the classified catalogue are the CLASSIFIED FILE of entries in systematic order, and the complementary alphabetical SUBJECT INDEX.

SUBJECT ENTRY is the basic unit of the subject catalogue. It consists of subject heading, description of document, and (except in bibliographies) location. In a book index or an alphabetical index to a classified catalogue, the description is not present. In the systematic file of a classified catalogue the heading may also be a location symbol.

SUBJECT HEADING is the statement of the subject of a document (or other chosen literary unit). It stands at the head of the entry, and its substance and form determine the structure and arrangement of the catalogue. In the two forms of alphabetical subject catalogue, the heading consists of words. Headings of more than one word may also include punctuation to which an arranging significance may be assigned. In the classified catalogue the heading consists of a classification symbol with or without its verbal equivalent. The phrase SUBJECT HEADING LANGUAGE embraces subject terms from which mere references are made to other subject terms, as well as subject headings as defined here.

NATURAL LANGUAGE refers to English alone. Particular statements made about natural language might need qualification for other languages.

FEATURE HEADING is the verbal part of the subject heading used in the systematic file in a classified catalogue. The feature heading is essentially a translation into words of the last digit in the classification symbol, but it can also be utilised to specify subjects for which no exact notation is provided in the classification scheme.

ENTRY WORD is the leading word of a subject heading in an alphabetically arranged catalogue or index.

SUBHEADING is the second or subsequent word in a verbal subject heading, separated from the preceding word by punctuation. The second word of a phrase (as 'Energy' in 'Free Energy') is not referred to as a subheading.

COMPOUND SUBJECT is a subject which requires more than one word to express its meaning in the heading. A compound subject may be either a phrase or a combination, the separate words of which are divided by punctuation.

COMPONENT is an individual constituent word in a compound subject heading.

REFERENCE is a direction from one heading to another in the same sequence.

An UPWARD REFERENCE is a direction from a less to a more comprehensive subject heading in an alphabetico-specific catalogue.

A DOWNWARD REFERENCE is a direction from a more to a less comprehensive heading in an alphabetico-specific catalogue.

A COLLATERAL REFERENCE in an alphabetico-specific catalogue links two headings belonging to the same hierarchical level, which are subsumed under a common immediate generic term, and would stand side by side if arranged in a classification scheme.

MECHANICAL SELECTOR is a subject catalogue incorporating a mechanism which searches the entries for a required subject. All mechanical selectors work on the principle that a searching or scanning device bearing, in code form, the subject of the enquiry is set to find a matching code in a store of subject coded entries. This became feasible with the appearance of punched card coding and sorting, but the vast potentialities of selectors have been associated with the development of the photoelectric cell and the computer type of electronic relay. Mechanical selectors as practical tools are still very much in their infancy, not because of insuperable problems on the engineering side, but because many questions still await solution on the pre-organisation both of the information which is required to store in the machine and of the content of enquiries. To a great extent these are the basic questions underlying the construction of any subject index or catalogue, for manual or mechanical operation. Hence their importance for libraries, and the relevance for them of library experience.

NEUTRALITY is a term used to describe a situation in subject cataloguing in which user preference cannot be invoked (either because it is unascertainable or because it does not exist) to justify one course of action over another. Most of the problems discussed in this book concern a neutral catalogue, and any suggestions made are subject to not being contrary to user preference or interest. Most catalogues of general libraries are preponderantly neutral in this sense. Special library practice can be more closely parallel to the habits and viewpoints of a homogeneous clientele, but complex subjects of equal interest to equally important user groups may produce neutral situations in special library subject cataloguing.

Where user habit and requirement is ascertainable with sufficient precision, there is, of course, no need for cataloguing rules of any kind.

The terms listed so far stand for ideas which pervade the book as a whole. Those which follow come into use only in the latter half of the book, and their meanings will in most cases be evident from the text. They are set down here for ease of reference and in order to forestall any possible misunderstanding as to the sense in which they are used. They need not be read until difficulties are met in the text.

A SCHEDULE is a list of terms, indented upon a page so as to show hierarchical relationship, which comprises the tables of a classification scheme. As used in this book it normally has no reference to the notation of the classification scheme.

FACET is employed here in a slightly wider sense than that of Dr. S. R. Ranganathan,[2] who established it as a technical term in classification studies. It is used here as a collective name for the series of terms (or subject concepts) produced when a subject is divided by a single characteristic. All the terms within a facet are related in the same manner to the subject concept which has been so divided. Fox, Dog, Fish, Spider, Bivalve are terms in one facet of Zoology. Migration, Hibernation, Protective Coloration are terms in a different facet. Facets themselves may often be divided into sub-facets.

CHAIN – also to be credited to Dr. Ranganathan – is a hierarchy of terms in a classification scheme, each term containing or including all those which follow it.

CHAIN PROCEDURE is a method, first propounded by Dr. Ranganathan, of constructing subject index entries, without permutation of components, by citing terms contained in particular chains.

A QUALIFIER is a subheading in a subject index which has been constructed by chain procedure.

BASIC ANALYSIS is the first stage in converting a classification symbol into a verbal subject heading for an alphabetico-specific catalogue. It consists of the citation in upward hierarchical order of the constituent elements of a composite subject.

QUALIFIED LIST is the phrase used to denote the second stage of the conversion of a class symbol to a verbal subject heading. It is produced by deleting False and Unsought links of the chain, and adding qualifiers to the remaining terms.

APPROACH TERM is the single word which the enquirer seeks in the catalogue, which he anticipates will lead him to a statement in subject heading language of a required compound subject.

HIERARCHICAL OR GENERIC SEARCH is an examination of entries under headings which constitute a chain. It is conducted in upward direction from the most to the least specific heading.

The course of a Hierarchical search may include what is termed a SUBSTITUTION GENERIC. This denotes a situation in the alphabetico-specific catalogue in which two headings each with the same number of subheadings represent concepts in hierarchical relationship. E.g.

> STRIP, Copper, Surface treatment
> STRIP, Copper, Electroplating.

SYSTEMATIC COLLATERAL SEARCH is an examination of entries under headings which, in a scheme of classification, would be co-ordinate with, and stand next to, each of the headings covered in the hierarchical search.

ALPHABETICAL COLLATERAL SEARCH is an examination of entries under headings alphabetically adjacent to, or in the vicinity of, the headings covered in the hierarchical search.

## NOTES AND REFERENCES

[1] Pettee, J. *Subject headings* (New York, 1946).
[2] See Ranganathan, S. R. *Prolegomena to library classification* (London, 1957), pp. 168–195.
    Palmer, B. I. & Wells, A. J. *Fundamentals of library classification* (London, 1951).
    Vickery, B. C. *Classification and indexing in science*. 2nd ed. (London, 1959), pp. 12–42, and 211–215.

# CHAPTER II

## SUBJECT RECORDING AND RECOVERY

A SUBJECT catalogue, in the somewhat extended sense in which the term is used in this book, is a device which enables an enquirer to find out which documents in a collection or list contain information on a particular required subject. Essentially it comprises a series of directions whereby the enquirer is led from the names of subjects to the names (or other identifying symbols, such as accession numbers) of documents which contain information on the respective subjects. The starting point of any such key to subject content must be a list of subject headings arranged in self-evident order, usually alphabetical. The terms in the alphabetical heading list may signpost the documents directly as in the dictionary catalogue; or indirectly, by way of a subject classification symbol as in the classified catalogue, or through a code pattern of holes, notches, photographic or magnetic spots representing a subject in a mechanical selector.[1]

### MANUAL AND MECHANICAL SUBJECT RETRIEVAL

Subject catalogues may be designed for direct manual and visual operation or for scrutiny by a mechanical searching and selecting device. This book will be concerned with the headings and structure of manually operated catalogues and indexes, and only incidentally with mechanical selector systems. However, it may be a profitable exercise to consider at this stage certain features of mechanical selectors which serve to throw into relief the basic operating principles of manually consulted catalogues. The question of intended operation by a human or machine[2] searcher will affect profoundly both the manner of arrangement of material in the catalogue as well as the depth of subject detail which can be recorded. Nevertheless the selecting mechanism is programmed by a human operator in response to an enquiry couched in natural language. Both types of subject catalogue, mechanical and manual, give rise to the problem of the re-expression of ideas, at first rendered in natural language, in a language form suitable for subject catalogue headings. The fact that in the mechanical selector subject data are coded as physical patterns of holes and spots, in no way absolves selector operators from the task of formulating the 'subject heading language'. In fact, the efforts now being made to rationalise the programming of mechanical selectors have stimulated thought and discussion on subject cataloguing generally. In the words of R. A. Fairthorne, 'It is the work behind automata, rather than automata themselves, that has value to libraries.'[3]

Mechanical selector methods also usefully dramatise what is involved in the consultation of a manually operated catalogue. In mechanical selection the enquiry is fed, in code form, into a scanning device which is thus set to select all similar codes encountered in the store of entries. In the manually operated catalogue the enquirer similarly tries to find reproduced as a subject heading the word or phrase which he has in mind as the name of the required subject. In both cases the symbols representing the enquiry must match that representing the subject content of the documents catalogued.

### SUMMARISATION IN SUBJECT CATALOGUING

No catalogue gives an exhaustive statement of all subjects in the documents concerned. This would not be possible without causing the headings for each document to rival the document itself in elaboration and complexity, and without raising the cost of cataloguing and catalogue consultation to a prohibitively high level. No document stored in a collection is informationally as valuable as that. However, the mechanical selector is much less restricted in this respect than the manually operated catalogue, on account of the small space occupied by a large number of entries and the high speed with which they can be inspected by the scanning mechanism. These physical advantages suggest that the appropriate role of the mechanical selector may be to store and retrieve, not summaries of documentary idea-content, such as subject headings may be said to be, but the total idea-content of each document. The potentialities of mechanical selectors for exhaustive recording and storing of information offer a reminder that the headings of manually operated subject catalogues and indexes are the result of summarisation of the document, or extraction from it, or a combination of both. For any given catalogue or index, summarisation and extraction must be based on consistent criteria. In practice we find that summarisation is governed by formal criteria, and extraction by intrinsic ones. The two basic processes of summarisation and extraction are exhibited in differing degrees in various kinds of indexes and catalogues. In the conventional index to a book, the indexer extracts certain words or phrases from the text, according to their importance to the subject or theme of the book. The special library cataloguer may extract from documentary material of all kinds, passages which fall within his library's specialty; he then assigns to the extracted passages subject headings which summarise their content. The subject cataloguer of a general library, or the compiler of a bibliography of general scope, has by the very fact of the generality of his subject field no intrinsic criterion to serve as a principle for extraction, as all the information in the documents must be considered as of equal importance. General library subject cataloguing is essentially summarisation. In making a summary one chooses a formal literary unit, such as sentence, paragraph, or, more usually, whole document. A good deal of the criticism levelled at traditional cataloguing by those concerned with mechanical selectors arises from failure to appreciate this. The fact that a record of the subjects of whole books fails to disclose the content of a particular paragraph emphasises the limitations of summarisation at that level, but does not necessarily invalidate the methods of summarisation employed.

In practice, of course, the principle of a summary subject heading per whole document is not adhered to quite rigidly. A book may be incapable of summarisation because it has no unity of content; it may be multi-topical, and require several entries. In classified catalogue practice, single subjects for which no unitary provision is made in the classification scheme used, are given multiple entry according to intrinsic subject criteria.

### CLASSIFICATION AND SUBJECT CATALOGUING

The operation here called summarisation, the abstraction of the overall idea embodied in the subject content of a given literary unit, besides being basic to most forms of subject cataloguing, is also the most important process in subject classification. The two disciplines only diverge at the subsequent phase in which the abstracted idea is reformulated by the subject cataloguer as a subject heading and by the classifier as a classification symbol. Both techniques provide answers to the question 'What is the subject of this document?' which are different in form alone.

The affinity between subject cataloguing and classification does not cease here. Every form of subject catalogue attempts to assist the enquirer by providing links between related subjects, and we shall see that as soon as we attempt to construct coherent and comprehensive systems of such links, we encounter classificatory ideas. We shall see also how classification has sometimes been employed to supply a basis for rationalising the word order of compound subject headings. No attempt is made here to respect a frontier which exists only in tradition and in professional examination syllabuses where, in the writer's view its abolition is long overdue.

## SUBJECT HEADING LANGUAGE IN THE ALPHABETICAL CATALOGUE

The teaching of the art of reducing to a single idea the content of a piece of literature is outside the scope of this book. It is allied to what is called 'comprehension' in language study and to abstracting in the technical sense. Indeed, a subject heading might be described as an abstract which merely records the overall concept covered by the document in question. This narrows the scope of the subsequent discussion almost entirely to questions of arrangement; both of the subject headed entries themselves, which may be said to constitute the structure of the catalogue; and of the component words within compound headings, which may be regarded as very nearly equivalent to the problem of subject heading language.

Attention will be focused primarily on the alphabetically arranged subject catalogue, including the subject index to a classified catalogue. That the special problems of the latter may throw useful light upon alphabetical subject catalogues generally is the main theme of the later chapters.

Throughout, the point of view will necessarily be that of a 'neutral' catalogue without bias to a particular subject. Many decisions in subject cataloguing practice can and should be made in the light of what is known about the clients of the library and their particular needs and points of view. To the extent that users can be categorised as homogeneous groups and their viewpoints determined, subject cataloguing problems do not exist. This book is concerned with residual problems which cannot be decided because the user preferences in respect of them are indeterminate. These problems naturally loom more largely in general than in special libraries, but they are not absent from the latter. It is not usually possible to say of every subject represented in a library that it is more relevant to the work and interests of one particular group of users than to others. The arguments to be presented and suggestions made are to be understood as applicable to neutral subject cataloguing situations. Where they conflict with the known needs of a preponderant group of users, the latter will obviously prevail.

Special library subject catalogue entries normally record smaller literary units than those of general libraries. Therefore the concepts requiring expression as subject headings are correspondingly more intricate in special libraries. Hence the problem of 'subject heading language' bears more hardly on the special library cataloguer, while for his opposite number in the general library the actual process of summarising is the more onerous part of the subject cataloguing task. This does not mean that the problem of 'subject heading language' is not of importance to general library cataloguers. It has become increasingly clear that existing subject catalogue techniques, as exemplified for instance, in the subject catalogues of the Library of Congress, are falling short even at their own summarisation level. They do not altogether adequately reveal the subject content of whole books: and in a communications-conscious era, when specialised knowledge is more frequently than hitherto finding its way into book form, it is at least doubtful if traditional methods can now be said to be efficient in libraries of any kind. Catalogue deficiencies in a general library are by no means self-revealing. When the enquirer draws a blank at the catalogue there is no basis for further check apart from the personal memory of the enquirer or of the library staff. In a library confined to a narrow sector of knowledge, manned by specialists in that sector, personal memory exercises a severer scrutiny on catalogue efficiency than is possible in a general library. If subject cataloguing seems especially problematic in special libraries at the present moment, it does not follow that all is well in general libraries.

There should be little need to lay emphasis on the key role of subject cataloguing in libraries. The potential usefulness of library materials cannot be exploited without it, once the library has grown beyond the point at which its contents are adequately at the recall of personal memory. The vast increase in the number of documents in every sphere of human activity, the increased complexity of the pattern of knowledge, and the accelerating development of new knowledge necessitate a foolproof method of access to records on any subject that may be required.

## NOTES AND REFERENCES

[1] cf. Vickery, B. C. *Structure of a connective index.* J. Docum. Vol. 6, 1950, pp. 140–151.

[2] cf. Vickery, B. C. *Some comments on mechanical selection.* Amer. Docum. Vol. 2, 1951, pp. 102–107.

[3] Fairthorne, R. A. *Automata and information.* J. Docum. Vol. 8, 1952, p. 172.

# CHAPTER III

## THE TWO-FOLD OBJECTIVE

ALL forms of subject catalogue have a two-fold objective; first, to enable an enquirer to identify documents on a given subject, and second, to make known the presence of material on allied subjects.

### LOCATION OF MATERIAL ON A PARTICULAR SUBJECT

The first part of this objective demands a set of subject headings which, as far as possible, match the terms likely to be in the minds of enquirers wishing to locate material on a subject.

This would be fairly simple to achieve if there were an uncomplicated one-to-one relationship between concepts and words: that is to say, if there were a single word corresponding to each separate concept and a single concept corresponding to each separate word. In fact, we have on the one hand concepts that can be rendered by any one of a number of words, and on the other hand concepts for which no single word equivalent exists in natural language.

Considering first the situation where the concept has several verbal equivalents, we are confronted by the fact that the same subject may be represented by different terms in the minds of different enquirers. Natural language uses synonyms as alternatives on diverse occasions, whereas in subject heading practice whenever a term is used, all its synonyms must be recorded at the same time.

The only way of being reasonably sure of gathering in all used synonyms of a term would be to examine all the literature of the subject and observe the usages of authors. This is practicable only in so far as the literature to be examined has already been classified in libraries, bibliographies, and lists of abstracts. With alphabetically arranged subject lists and bibliographies there is always the possibility that the literature may be grouped under one of the synonymous terms which the cataloguer is attempting to discover. Unless he happens to recognise it as such, it will beg the very question to which an answer is sought. If we do not know in advance all the synonyms, no alphabetical-verbal subject grouping will give us certain access to all the literature we need to inspect to discover what the synonyms are. In order to avoid this logically closed circle, we need some method of collocating the literature by subject that does not depend upon words. In the last resort classification is the only tool which reveals the full variety of names under which a single concept may be discussed.

Self-contained alphabetical subject catalogues – that is to say those which refer directly to the names of the documents, and not, as for instance, the subject index to a classified catalogue, to a location number in another list – are called on to resolve a further problem in connection with synonyms. For, although the complete range of synonyms of a given term must be entered in the catalogue, it is economically prohibitive to give full information under each. It therefore becomes necessary to select from the set of synonyms a preferred term under which alone particulars of the document are given. Each of the remaining synonyms carries a reference to the subject heading so chosen.

Here again the basis of choice must be observation of the usage of writers on the subject. In default of direct mass-observation of the habits of enquirers, the cataloguer is obliged to follow the terminological preferences of the majority of writers on the subject. There are, of course, occasions when no such preferences are discernable; indeed in many subject fields (and not only newly emerging ones) there is little evidence of agreement even on the meaning of terms, still less on which synonyms are to be preferred. Circumstances may well arise, therefore, when the cataloguer is obliged to choose one of a number of equally suitable synonyms.

A question which may reasonably be put is: If various writers use differing terms for the same subject, how can the cataloguer, dependent as he is on author's usage, altogether avoid entering the same subject under different headings? The best safeguard is to be found in utilising the results of classification. Just as classification can be employed to reveal synonyms, so also it can be used to ensure that no two synonyms can masquerade in the catalogue as separate and distinct subjects. Provided that the documents are classified as fully as the classification scheme allows, a subject heading authority list in classified order will virtually eliminate the chance of entering the same subject under different synonymous terms. A variety of terms entered in the authority list under the same class symbol may, of course, simply indicate that the classification scheme needs expansion at this point, but at least the terms can be checked against one another as possible synonyms. The less arbitrary the classification scheme, the greater is the degree of protection offered by this method.

In a scheme, such as the Colon Classification, where the recognition of 'facets' permits the close control of composite subjects, the safeguard obtainable against entry under synonym is almost absolute. Alphabetically arranged authority lists, giving references from synonyms, are helpful in so far as they are the result of an adequate inspection of the literature on each subject made possible by classification.

The elimination of dual location under synonymous headings is the less formidable of the two main problems involved in adapting natural language for the purposes of subject headings. We may now turn to the opposite situation, to which reference has already been made, where there is no single word which represents the concept. Such concepts are expressed in natural language by combinations of words constituting phrases. New concepts are normally rendered by means of phrases, and only a minority later acquire single word status.

Unfortunately there are certain disadvantages in the use of phrases as subject headings. Enquirers consulting catalogues and indexes attempt to formulate sought topics as single words, even in cases where a phrase would be needed in natural language. Hence the well established principle that when a concept can be cited either as a single word or a phrase, the single word is to be preferred as subject heading. Phrase subject headings create uncertainty in the minds of enquirers on three separate counts. In the first place there is uncertainty as to the order in which the words of the phrase are cited in the subject heading. Does the heading retain the order of natural language or are the words transposed? As will be seen in later chapters, there is no single solution to this problem. A thoroughgoing rule either to use natural language order always, or inversion always, leads to unsatisfactory results.

Secondly, phrase headings introduce an element of uncertainty as to filing order which does not arise with single word headings. What is the filing order of the space between the words of the phrase, in relation to the sequence A to Z? Is the space to be ignored in filing? The differences in filing order depending upon the cataloguer's decision on these questions are far from negligible. It requires a certain amount of conscious deliberation on the part of the enquirer to discover whether the principle of arrangement is 'word by word' (with the space preceding letter 'a' in ordinal sequence) or 'letter by letter' (with the space ignored in arrangement), and particularly in card or sheaf catalogues where a single entry occupies a whole unit of stationery, relevant material may be missed because the enquirer has made a wrong assumption as to the principle of arrangement in use.

Finally, there is uncertainty as to which form of phrase will represent the concept as subject heading. Nearly all phrases consisting of an adjective followed by a noun, or a noun used adjectivally followed by a noun (as for instance 'Colonial Administration' or 'Child Psychology'), can also be rendered as a more extended phrase consisting of a noun followed by a relational word (or words), followed by a further noun (as 'Administration of Colonies' or 'Psychology of Children'). Both forms are permissible and common in ordinary language.

It may be suggested as a possible solution to this difficulty that the shortened form of phrase without the relational word should be used consistently throughout the catalogue. Unfortunately natural language acknowledges a shortened form in a limited number of cases only. Thus while 'Child Psychology' is a fully acceptable derivation from natural language, 'Infant Psychology' is rather rare, and 'Boy Psychology' would be an entirely artificial heading without precedent in natural language. Similarly while 'Animal Psychology' is admitted in natural language, 'Chimpanzee Psychology' would be, to say the least, unusual, though there is a sizeable body of writing on the latter subject. These examples are all intelligible with slight mental effort, but the effect of the compounds which have no counterparts in natural language is likely to startle and disconcert even the more enterprising enquirer. Artificial phrases of more than two components are likely to be even more disconcerting and may give rise to difficulties of comprehension.

The reverse solution would be to cite all phrases with the relational word included, giving such headings as 'Psychology of Children', 'Psychology of Chimpanzees', 'Psychology of Animals, etc.' This is a better solution than the use of artificial phrases. The headings here are taken from natural language, and the vast majority of concepts which cannot be expressed in a single word may be rendered in this form. However, there are a certain number of adjective-and-noun phrases, particularly when the noun is abstract in character, which will not readily transform into a phrase of the noun relational word noun pattern, without the use of a second noun not found in the original adjective-noun phrase. For instance 'Free Verse' and 'Foreign Relations', would have to be rendered 'Verse Free as to Rhyme and Metre' and 'Relations between Foreign Countries' in order to conform to the proposed pattern.

It appears that we cannot remove the enquirer's uncertainty as to which of the two basic phrase forms he should use in formulating his subject. It is not practicable to adopt in the catalogue either the shortened form of phrase (e.g. 'Child Psychology'), or the extended form (e.g. 'Psychology of Children') exclusively. Even if we consistently prefer one form as a matter of policy, there will always be some subjects which can only be clearly expressed in the other form. However, there are fewer subjects which cannot clearly be expressed in the extended form than in the shortened form, so the use of the extended form where possible is perhaps the better policy.

A subheaded form of subject heading (as 'Colonies, Administration', or 'Children, Psychology') has some advantages over phrase form as a method of rendering subjects which cannot be expressed in a single word. While in itself the subheaded form makes no contribution to the problem of word order within the subject heading, it does by means of the separating device which it inserts between words proclaim that the alphabetising is by the 'word by word' method. The gain in terms of general clarity and enquirers' confidence in handling the catalogue is not to be underrated.

The subheaded form can, as the example given shows, replace both of the possible alternative forms of phrase heading, thus obviating the enquirer's uncertainty as to the form in which the subject should be couched in order to match with a possible heading.

All extended phrases which include a relational word (or words) can be given in the subheaded form. Thus 'Embouchure, Oboe', or 'Oboe, Embouchure'. Where the number of elementary concepts in the combination does not exceed two, the relational word can usually be omitted altogether from the subheaded form.

Where there is a greater number of components to be cited, it may be necessary to include a relational word to avoid ambiguity, as in 'Owls, Pests, Control by', which, without the final preposition, might be understood as 'Control of Owls as Pests'.

However in these cases the relational word is relegated to an insignificant position in the heading, where it exercises little influence upon filing order. For the most part it is sufficient to cite the component concepts, leaving the nature of the relationship to be understood by the enquirer.

Phrases in the shortened form, consisting of noun (used adjectivally) followed by a second noun, as 'Child Psychology', can normally be entered in the subheaded form with a minimum of alteration. Some slight difficulty may sometimes arise from the use of plural forms of single words. Thus 'Child Psychology' would become 'Children, Psychology', though this would scarcely inconvenience users as long as the catalogue contains no heading commencing with the singular form 'Child'. In dictionary catalogues, or combined indexes to classified catalogues, where titles and subjects are combined in one sequence, it would be necessary to have a reference from the singular to the plural form in such a case.

We have already mentioned a class of adjective-noun phrases which will not easily be turned into an extended phrase of the noun relational word noun pattern. These phrases are similarly resistant to conversion into a subheaded form of subject heading. In other cases, particularly where the adjective is derived from a reasonably concrete noun, it is possible to use this noun as the first word of a subheaded subject heading. Thus 'Colonial Administration' and 'Molecular Structure' can be rendered as 'Colonies, Administration' and 'Molecules, Structure'. On the whole it would seem to be desirable as a matter of practical policy to render phrases as subheadings of single word headings as far as possible, retaining the phrase form only for those adjective and noun phrases which cannot be adapted.

It may be pointed out that the problem of entry of concepts for which there is no corresponding single word is often less acute in a library of limited subject field than in a general library. Combinations of words in natural language provide a semantic context for one another. In special library practice the limited subject field *is* the semantic context within which single word headings are assumed to be standing.

Thus in a library limited to chemical subjects, 'Compounds' would represent a concept which in a general library catalogue would require the heading 'Chemistry, Compounds' or 'Compounds, Chemistry'. The very words the enquirer expects to find as headings will depend in part upon his conception of the subject field of the library. The ordinary habits of informal discourse provide a close analogy here. When addressing a professional colleague, a librarian will, for example, refer to time sheets, issues, withdrawals and so on, knowing that he will be understood. Discussing the same topics with a lay person he will be more apt to specify 'staff time sheets', 'book issues', and 'stock withdrawals'. The mutually understood contextual field determines what words may be omitted. So also with the limited or general subject of a subject catalogue.

### LOCATION OF MATERIAL ON RELATED SUBJECTS

We can now pass on to a consideration of the second part of the function of a subject catalogue, the signalling of subjects related to the one which is being looked up. This must be attempted because an enquirer may wish to survey all the available material on a broad subject field.

Thus, for instance, he may try to locate all material on Civil Engineering. There will perhaps be entries under that heading, but these are merely documents on civil engineering in general. The catalogue also contains further material scattered under the headings 'Piles, Driving', 'Structures, Engineering', 'Bridges', 'Roads, Construction', 'Railways, Construction', 'Hydraulic Engineering'. All of these are included in Civil Engineering. The problem is to bring them to the attention of the enquirer at 'Civil Engineering'. The obvious solution is to insert directions in the form of 'see also' references

> Civil Engineering, *see also* Piles, Driving
> Bridges, etc.

The same piece of mechanism will also serve an enquirer of another kind; namely, the person who though actually needing material on a restricted subject, nevertheless attempts to find it under the name of a wider subject, either because he has not narrowed the topic down in his own mind or because he expects that the catalogue or index will group matter into broad subject fields. In this case also, 'see also' references directed *downwards* from general subject to less general subjects will provide what is required.

Let us consider another situation. An enquirer has approached the librarian for assistance in finding some information on, say, Clover Leaf Road Junctions. The librarian commences a systematic search, starting, perhaps, under 'Roads'. Not finding any subheadings here under 'Intersections' or 'Junctions', he tries the documents under 'Roads, Design'. The desired information not being given, he next tries the more general material under 'Roads, Construction', again without results. Where is he to go from here? His line of search now lies in two directions, he must search the material under all subjects which *include* Road Construction, proceeding stage by stage to more comprehensive subjects, taking in turn 'Civil Engineering', 'Engineering', 'Technology', and 'General Encyclopædias'. Books under any of these headings may contain a chapter or paragraph giving the information needed on clover leaf junctions. His second line of search is directed towards collateral subjects. Two subjects are said to be collateral when they share or operate with a certain number of common principles and problems. A collateral of 'Roads, Construction' is 'Permanent Way, Engineering', material under which might conceivably be relevant to the enquiry.

In order to permit such a search to be carried out, the catalogue must be equipped with 'see also' references from restricted to general

subjects in an *upwards* direction, and collateral subjects should preferably be linked together in both directions.

The signposting of related subjects by means of 'see also' references is
the characteristic device of what may be termed the alphabetico-
specific subject catalogue. This form of catalogue, when incorporated
in a single sequence with author and title entries, constitutes the dictionary catalogue.

There is one other way, beside the use of connective references, by
which subject relationship may be indicated in catalogues. This is by
physically assembling the entries on related topics. Instead of telling the
enquirer 'Office Organisation *see also* Typewriting' in the alphabetical
sequence, we file the entries on Office Organisation next to those on
Typewriting. This principle of collocating entries on related subjects
has given rise to the classified catalogue and the alphabetico-classed
catalogue.

Specific alphabetical entry designed to give the enquirer immediate
access to his subject (assuming he has thought of the catalogue's preferred synonym) is incompatible with the assembly of entries on
related subjects. The alphabetico-specific catalogue arranges headings
by their affinities of spelling, the classified and the alphabetico-classed
forms arrange their entries by affinities of meaning. If we arrange by
affinities of meaning, it becomes necessary to provide a supplementary
alphabetical list of subject headings which will direct the enquirer to
the place in the catalogue under which entries on the desired subject
have been filed. In other words, the enquirer must make two references
in every case. He must first consult the supplementary alphabetical list,
and then refer to the place in the catalogue to which the entry in the
alphabetical list has referred him. It is on this point, the value of direct
access versus display of entries on related subjects, that the great
debates[1] on the respective merits of the dictionary and classified
catalogues have turned.

It is clear that some enquirers demand material on a specific subject,
while others want to collect all available information over a field embracing a variety of subjects. Neither form of catalogue will serve both
groups equally well. Furthermore there are imponderables in the claim
of both sides. How large a proportion of dictionary catalogue enquirers
are directed first to synonyms used only as reference headings? How
far does the classified catalogue really succeed in assembling the entries
on related topics?

No attempt will be made here to answer these questions decisively, but in connection with the latter query, it should be noticed that of the two alternative mechanisms, the system of connective references and the collocation of entries on related subjects, the system of references alone can be made to reveal an unlimited range and variety of subject relationships. Indeed it will later be argued that the very facility with which references can be made to link subjects has helped to turn the dictionary catalogue into an unreliable tool. Had the reference mechanism been subject to obvious restrictions, cataloguers might well have been stimulated to develop means of overcoming them, if not completely, at least systematically. Dictionary cataloguing is often too arbitrary, too dependent on personal momentary recollection, to achieve adequate linkage of related subjects, but in theory its capacities in this respect are unlimited.

The method of showing subjects as related by bringing them together in the catalogue has certain severe limitations. As the catalogue is a sequence, no subject can be related in this manner to more than two others: namely to its collateral which precedes it and that which follows it. However, the aggregate of a series of collaterals is in generic relation to each of them, and in classification systems and the classified catalogue two kinds of subject relationships (between generic and its specifics, and between collaterals) are telescoped into a single dimension simply by placing the generic subject at the beginning of its group of constituent collateral subjects.

Thus in the sequence

1 TRANSPORT
2 AIR TRANSPORT
3 WATER TRANSPORT
4 LAND TRANSPORT
5 ROAD TRANSPORT

We have 3 collaterals (2) to (4), generic-specific relationship between (1) and all the rest, and also between (4) and (5).

In classification schedules we make use of the second dimension of the page, and symbolise the different relationships by indentation

TRANSPORT
    AIR TRANSPORT
    WATER TRANSPORT
    LAND TRANSPORT
        ROAD TRANSPORT

We can do the same in an index consisting of headings and location references. For a catalogue in page form the generic-specific relationship is expressed by typographical differentiation. In a card catalogue recourse must be had to distinction by guide cards bearing tabs of varying lateral position and colour.

By the method of assembly or collocation, we can show up to two collateral relatives of a given subject, and one hierarchical series of class terms. This is not adequate for efficient handling of subject enquiries. A topic may have more than two close collateral relatives and may well be a member of more than one hierarchical series. Cross references between separated parts of the classified catalogue may be used in an attempt to make good the deficiency, but in this the classified cataloguer is scarcely in a better plight than his colleague of the dictionary catalogue with his freedom to make 'see also' references. In neither case is there a criterion or principle upon which to proceed nor any method of checking that all necessary subject relationships have been exhibited. All that can be said is that, within the limits of the classification scheme used, the classified catalogue goes further in organising the exhibition of subject relationship than does the alphabetico-specific form.

Like the classified catalogue, the alphabetico-classed[2] catalogue assembles material on related subjects, at the cost of abandonment of direct access to a specific subject heading.

A catalogue of this kind consists of an alphabetical sequence of mutually exclusive broad subject headings, under each of which appears a further alphabetical sequence of subheadings. The process of alphabetical subdivision can be carried down to the degree of minuteness required by the material being catalogued. The following illustrates the kind of pattern produced:

```
ARCHÆOLOGY
    - CLASSICAL
    - MEDIÆVAL
    - PREHISTORIC
        - BRONZE AGE
        - CHRONOLOGY
            - RADIO-CARBON
        - CROMLECHS
        - EARTHWORKS
        - IRON AGE
ARCHITECTURE
    - ABBEYS
    - ARCHES
    - CHURCHES
        - ROOFS
            - BOSSES
```

- FACTORIES
- HISTORY
- HOUSES
- ROOFS
- SCHOOLS ]

As will be seen from this example class hierarchical relationships between subjects are expressed, but the alphabetical subarrangement precludes the demonstration of relationships between collaterals.

It also precludes logical arrangement of the subjects at a particular hierarchical level. The two prehistoric epochs are separated by the general topic Prehistoric Chronology, and by two varieties of remains which may or may not have any connection with either. Similarly under Architecture parts of buildings are not segregated from kinds of buildings. The bizarre appearance is of course an effect of the attempt to exploit both subject grouping and alphabetical arrangement at the same time. For all subjects except those chosen as main classes the enquirer must make two consultations. In the first place he refers to the specific name of the desired subject, and here he finds a reference giving him the topic's location under its appropriate hierarchical heading (e.g. RADIO-CARBON DATING – PREHISTORY – *see* ARCHÆOLOGY – PREHISTORIC – CHRONOLOGY – RADIO-CARBON).

These references from specific subject names correspond to the subject index entries of a classified catalogue, but thanks to its alphabetical basis the alphabetico-classed catalogue does not need to keep its main catalogue and supporting references in two separate parts. The psychological advantage, from the enquirer's point of view, is considerable.

In the preceding paragraphs we have seen how the structure of catalogues is determined by their employment of one of two possible methods of showing subject relationship. A purely alphabetical arrangement of headings has as a corollary complete reliance upon connective references. The alternative mechanism – the physical assembly of subject headings related by meaning – necessitates partial (in the case of the alphabetico-classed catalogue) or complete (in the case of the classified catalogue) abandonment of alphabetical structure as far as the main catalogue is concerned. We have seen, however, that the alphabetico-classed and classified forms both require a supplementary alphabetical list of specific subject references. It has also been noticed that the alphabetico-specific and the classified forms are each preeminently suited for answering two different types of enquiry.

To attempt to evaluate one form against the other is probably fruitless, and in any case raises issues of subordinate importance. The problems of greater moment are those which the three forms of catalogue share with one another; for the problem of devising a coherent integrated plan or pattern of subject relationship[3] afflicts the alphabetico-specific catalogue just as the problem of how best to express compound specific subjects is urgently relevant to the alphabetico-classed and classified forms.

None of the three forms succeeds in by-passing problems which, at first sight, seem to be applicable only to the other two. Historically it was the last-mentioned problem in connection with the dictionary catalogue or alphabetico-specific index that exercised the attention of cataloguers first. In the next two chapters we shall consider some notable attempts to devise a rational procedure for rendering compound subjects as catalogue or index headings. In these attempts the further problem of expressing subject relationship was always in the background, but it was tacitly assumed to be an intuitive art, incapable of being reduced to rule or passed on to others by ordinary methods of communication.

## NOTES AND REFERENCES

[1] E.g. Quinn, J. H. *Library cataloguing* (London, 1913), pp. 19–32.

Pollard, A. F. & Bradford, S. C. *Inadequacy of the alphabetical subject index* (ASLIB Report of Proceedings, 7th Conference, 1930), pp. 39–54.

Bradford, S. C. *Documentation* (London, 1953), pp. 56–61.

[2] For a brief description of the alphabetico classed catalogue and some of its variants see Cranshaw, J. *The alphabetico-classed catalogue and its near relatives.* Library Assistant. Vol. 30, 1937, pp. 202–211.

[3] See also Vickery, B. C. *Structure of a connective index.* J. Docum. Vol. 6, 1950, pp. 140–151.

## Comparative structure of the three forms of catalogue

| PROBLEM | MECHANISM AVAILABLE | | |
|---|---|---|---|
| | *Alphabetico-specific form* | *Classified form* | *Alphabetico-classed form* |
| 1 Access to correctly formulated request | Direct to subject entry | Indirect via subject index | Indirect via 'see' references for all topics not main headings |
| 2 Synonyms | 'See' reference | As above | As above |
| 3 Hierarchical relationship. Generic-to-specific | 'See also' reference | Collocation of entries | Collocation of entries |
| 4 Hierarchical relationship. Specific-to-generic | 'See also' reference (None or few in dictionary catalogue practice) | Collocation of entries | Collocation of entries |
| 5 Collateral relationship | (a) 'See also' reference (b) Limited accidental collocation | (a) Collocation of entries to limited extent (b) Limited collocation in subject index | Limited accidental collocation of 'see' references |

| *Illustrative example* | | | |
|---|---|---|---|
| 1 Access to correctly formulated request | RADIO ENGINEERING | Radio engineering 621.384 | Radio engineering 'see' Communications – Radio |
| 2 Synonyms | WIRELESS 'see' RADIO | Wireless engineering 621.384 | Wireless engineering 'see' Communications – Radio |
| 3 Hierarchical relationship. Generic-to-specific | COMMUNICATIONS ENGINEERING 'see also' RADIO ENGINEERING | (Collocation in classified file) 621.38 – Communications 621.384 – Radio | (Collocation) Communications Communications – Radio |
| 4 Hierarchical relationship. Specific-to-Generic | RADIO ENGINEERING 'see also' COMMUNICATIONS ENGINEERING | Collocation in classified file as above | Collocation as above |
| 5 Collateral relationship | RADIO ENGINEERING 'see also' TELEGRAPHY | (a) Collocation in classified file 621.382 – Telegraphy 621.384 – Radio (b) Accidental collocation in subject index Radio engineering 621.384 Radio programmes 791.4 | Accidental collocation of references Radio engineering 'see' Communications – Radio Radio programmes 'see' Entertainment – Radio |

# CHAPTER IV

## TOWARDS SYSTEMISATION

IN the historical development of any craft there is always a well-marked stage at which a line of intuitive and empirically minded practitioners is brought to an abrupt end by someone who succeeds in rationalising the best current practice into a few general principles which can thereafter be applied consciously.

The year 1876 and the name Charles Ammi Cutter mark such a turning point in the history of subject cataloguing. In that year there appeared the first edition of Cutter's *Rules for a Dictionary Catalog*.[1] In about twenty-five pages of rules and comments Cutter virtually laid the foundations of subject cataloguing for the next three-quarters of a century. Not that his prescriptions have commanded general acceptance. The most influential of all dictionary catalogues – that of the Library of Congress – has only partially followed his principles. Yet because the *Rules* isolated the chief issues in alphabetical subject cataloguing and because Cutter left no intellectual successor capable of advancing from the point at which he stopped, his influence has endured long into a period in which vast changes in the form, scope, and social significance of literary records would otherwise have rendered it obsolete. Apart from J. Kaiser, S. R. Ranganathan and J. E. L. Farradane, whose contributions will be examined in detail later, subsequent generations of indexers and cataloguers have had little of substance to add. Cutter addressed himself to three principal problems. The first of these dealt with the implications of specific subject entry; the other two were concerned with subject headings consisting of more than one word, where the name of the subject is a phrase or where the subject of the book is a composite of subject name and locality name. In contrast to his more cautious interpreters, Cutter committed himself to definite rulings in each case. But it is clear from his appended comments that he was not always himself convinced by his own rulings.

### CUTTER'S CONCEPTION OF SPECIFIC ENTRY

On specific subject entry Cutter says (Rule 106): "Enter a work under its subject heading, not under the heading of the class which includes that subject." This sounds simple and straightforward, especially against our later background of detailed bibliographical classification. But if we understand the rule to mean that the subject heading is, as it were, to be made to measure the subject of the book, to fit the individual case, we are speedily disillusioned by the comment which follows the rule.

"Some subjects", explains Cutter, "have no name. They are spoken of by a phrase or phrases not definite enough to be used as a heading . . . it is not always easy to decide what is a distinct subject." If a book's subject is not "distinct", it is after all to have a class subject heading.

To appreciate fully Cutter's viewpoint on this we must bear in mind the half century which now separates him from us. The expression "distinct subject" had more meaning to Cutter and his contemporaries than it can have to us. At that time knowledge still consisted of a number of accepted spheres of thought, each comfortably separate from the others. "Subjects" were islands of knowledge separated from one another by oceanic voids. This was a great convenience and aid to tidy minds, no longer, alas, available. In our day the various islands have become so thoroughly interconnected that it is often very difficult to see any ocean at all. In fact, the geographical metaphor has to give way to a biological one. Any subject may impinge upon almost any other and the chances are that such a union will produce a brand-new offspring.

New subjects are being generated around us all the time, and while subjects may still be more or less distinct, there can be no hard and fast separation of the "distinct" subjects from the others.

Every subject which is sufficiently distinct to be treated in literary record is presumably capable of being expressed as a subject heading. The author must necessarily give it a name of some kind. If the name is a clumsy phrase it remains the indexer's or cataloguer's task to reduce it to usable subject heading form. Cutter cites "Movements of fluids in plants" as an example of an indistinct subject which he would be forced to enter under the non-specific heading "Botany, Physiological". Although, as he makes clear a few sentences further on, he mentally relates this subject to the idea of "circulation", he declined to use as specific heading "Plants, Circulation". Apparently in 1876 circulation or translocation of plant fluids was not one of the established subjects. In the course of the same comment Cutter makes it clear that even in his day it was sometimes hard to determine whether a subject was "established" or otherwise.

Briefly, there are two possible conceptions of specific subject entry.

The one favoured by Cutter envisages a set of stock subjects, under one of which each book had to be accommodated. If the subject matter of a book is more restricted in scope than any of the stock terms, then the book must be placed under the most restricted stock term which contains its subject, just as the purchaser of ready-made clothing buys the nearest larger stock size to his actual size. The whole difficulty is that no definite criterion can be adduced to determine what shall be in the stock list of subjects. While it is true that some subjects are more "established" than others, there are infinite gradations and no fixed demarcation of the "unestablished" is possible.

Among cataloguers, and teachers and students of cataloguing who follow the conception of the stock subject list, there can only be interminable and inconclusive argument whenever the first book on a new subject appears, as to whether the latter is sufficiently "distinct", "established", or "definite" to have a subject heading. A similar dilemma lies behind the query, "How specific must the specific topic be?"[2]

### AN ALTERNATIVE CONCEPTION OF SPECIFIC ENTRY

The alternative conception, advocated here, is that of the subject-heading made to measure, the subject heading co-extensive with the subject of the book. By devising the subject heading to fit the subject of the book precisely, we by-pass all questions of whether the subject is established, and how specific should headings be. The question of "grouping titles topically", which Cutter advocates in Rule 340, does not arise, because, as every subject will have been fully specified at the time of cataloguing, there will be no further scope or occasion for sub-division by subject. The case which Cutter makes out in the comment on Rule 340 for the utility of topical grouping might equally well be invoked for full subject specification, irrespective of whether the subject has a "definite" name or otherwise. However, Cutter's use of the term "subdivision" in this connection is advised. He was thinking in terms of classification into the main divisions of the subject given in the heading rather than of exact subject specification in all cases. He was being consistent with his own caveat against specific entry for subjects "without a definite name".

The point here, however, is that Cutter rejected the view that subsequences under the subject heading produced forbidding complications for the enquirer. On the contrary, exact specification by leaving under the general heading that which is alone generally on that subject, helps the enquirer. Cutter might perhaps have been reminded that this consideration applies equally to the enquirer for general material on "Botany, Physiological", who found there embedded a book on the specialised topic of movement of plant fluids.

The conception of subject headings-to-measure would result in the following redraft of the specific subject rule.

"Enter a work under the heading which expresses its subject precisely. Subjects whose names cannot be expressed in a single word or customary phrase consisting of adjective followed by a noun are to be specified exactly by a compound heading consisting of more than one word. The entry word in such cases will be a class-term relative to the specific subject. It will be followed by the further term (or terms) as subheadings. The meaning of the heading and subheading in combination must be unambiguous and self-explanatory."

The following examples illustrate how the rule would result in practice:

| | |
|---|---|
| Aluminium, Machining | Mouth, Histology |
| Gases, Kinetic Theory | Flats, Architecture |
| Floods, Social Relief | Distillation, Chemical Technology |
| Marriage, Psychology | Algae, Ecology |
| Coal Mines, Fires | |

### COMPONENT ORDER IN COMPOUND HEADINGS

In permitting the use of subheadings as a means of specifying subjects which cannot be named in a single word or phrase, we are left with one important problem. If, for instance, Psychology of Marriage is the subject in question, should we supply the heading 'Marriage, Psychology', or 'Psychology, Marriage'. Compound headings of any kind raise the important question of the order in which the constituent parts are to be cited. Which term, in effect, is to be the all-important entry word?

Although Cutter did not use subheadings in the way suggested here, he admitted compound phrase headings, where the phrase was sufficiently established by custom, and in Rules 174 and 175, he considers how the constituent words of such phrases are to be ordered in the heading. Finally he reaches the following decision:

"Enter a compound subject name by its first word, inverting the phrase only where some other word is decidedly more significant or is often used alone with the same meaning as the whole name."

The operative word here is "decidedly". Nearly all phrases are to be used as they stand.

Cutter comments defensively upon this rule, anticipating the charge of vagueness and apparent arbitrariness in operation. Repeatedly his adherence to the notion of "distinct" subjects leads him into difficulties. "A man might plausibly assert that Ancient History is a distinct subject. . . ."[3] He might indeed!

He considers and rejects the alternative possibility that phrases consisting of an adjective followed by a noun, might be always inverted to bring the noun into the leading position. Such a rule would have the merit of rigid consistency, but Cutter has no difficulty in demonstrating how frequently the noun is of minor significance in a phrase of this sort. It is a pity that he is not content to let a good case stand on its own merits. For he attempts a highly questionable theoretical justification for his rule, on the ground that "the noun in most cases expresses a class and the adjective limits the noun and makes the name that of a subclass. . . . In Comparative Anatomy, Capital Punishment, the noun is the name of several subjects, one of whose subdivisions is indicated by the adjective. And Comparative, Capital have only this limiting power; they do not imply any general subject. But ancient history may be viewed not only in this way . . . but also as equivalent to Antiquity; History . . . here then we choose Ancient as the heading on the principle of Rule 165 (i.e. the specific entry rule discussed above)." The argument seems to have petered inconclusively away.[4]

A variant of the same argument is used by Cutter to support his decision to enter under locality rather than subject in cataloguing a work on a subject limited to a particular locality (as Agriculture of Canada). In Rules 104 and 105, after reluctantly rejecting double entry as resulting in too great a profusion of entries, he concludes "A work dealing with a general subject with reference to a place is to be entered under the place, with merely a reference from the subject". One is inclined to ask what is meant by "general subject" here. Are we being again invited to agree upon another stock list – this time of "general subjects"? Two lists of "subdivisions" under locality headings are given with Rule 343, but as these lists each end in "etc.", and exclude some subjects such as Vases, Gems, Painting, for which local entry is recommended in the comment on Rule 165, we cannot assume that they comprise the general subjects Cutter had in mind.

Furthermore they are only meant to be used as subdivision headings where a large number of titles accumulates under a local heading. Where there are a few entries under (say) Japan, a book on Japanese Buddhism would presumably be entered simply under the heading Japan, with the reference 'Buddhism *see* Japan'. This is assuming that Buddhism is regarded as a "general subject". If it is not so regarded, it would then apparently be entered under Buddhism.

Cutter attempted to justify his preference for entry under locality by reasoning similar to that which he used to support his rule for compound subject names. The dictionary catalogue, went his argument, when confronted by a class and an individual as possible entry words, chose the latter. A place is individual and a subject is a class, therefore entry should be under place.

It is in connection with locality-with-topic-headings that Cutter makes his only direct reference to the possibility of specifying by means of subheadings, as opposed to grouping by classificatory subdivisions. In the comment on Rule 343 he says "It may be asked why we do not divide them (i.e. subject headings) still more (following out the dictionary plan fully) so as to have divisions under country like "Liliaceae", "Cows", "Horses". In a library of 200,000 books, arrangement in classes is as well suited to quick reference and avoids the loss of room occasioned by numerous headings". (Evidently he was confining his argument here to the printed catalogue.) He continues "With few books minute division has a very incomplete appearance, specialities occurring only here and there, and most of the titles being only those of general works". One might suppose this to be all the more reason why the rare speciality should be pin-pointed among the obscuring multitude of general works. However, the comment ends with a near volte face, "A card catalogue should have more thorough division than can be put into print – because it must look into the future".

### UNIFORM RULES AND CUSTOMARY USAGE

As Cutter himself rightly stressed, subject headings should as far as possible reproduce the customary use of names of subjects. The ideal to be aimed at is to use the terms that the average enquirer would employ in discussing the subject with himself, for this is virtually what he does in considering where to look in the catalogue. For subjects on which there is no customary usage, or where this cannot be ascertained, the best that the cataloguer can do is to proceed on self-explanatory and uniform lines. In other words, when there is no customary usage to follow, the cataloguer can best serve the enquirer by uniformity of method and decision based on a few all-embracing rules.

Upon this last point rests the whole justification for the alphabetico-specific catalogue, for it is known that many enquirers use a class-term approach in the first place. Despite this, the alphabetico-specific catalogue uses specific terms, because of the sheer difficulty (both for the cataloguer and the enquirer) of deciding under which of its possible hierarchical class-terms a specific subject is to be entered. We may know perhaps that many enquirers who really want material on Electro-acoustics, actually turn first to some generic term. But which generic term? Is it Communications Engineering, or Electrical Engineering, or just Engineering? A subject usually has several generic levels, but only one specific level. We adopt the term representing the unique specific level, because we do not know which of the various generic terms the enquirer is likely to approach. The principle of specific entry offers a simple and clear-cut operational rule for the cataloguer and enquirer alike.

## THE TWO INDEPENDENT OPERATIONS IN SUBJECT HEADING TECHNIQUE

The difficulty and confusion in Cutter's thinking about subject headings arises from his intermittent failure to distinguish between the criteria applicable to a complete subject heading on the one hand and to an entry word on the other. His specific subject rule 106 seems to apply only to cases where the entry word is the complete subject heading.

He fails to distinguish two separate stages in subject cataloguing a work for the alphabetico-specific catalogue. The first stage is the naming of the work's specific subject, the second is the selection of a particular part of a compound name to serve as entry word. It is not possible to derive from the specific subject rule a further principle to enable us to say which part of the subject heading shall be the entry word. It does not follow that because the adjective in an adjective-and-noun phrase limits the noun, the former must be the entry word. If this line of argument were to be taken seriously, we should expect to find its implication embodied in a fully comprehensive rule, without the proviso actually placed in Rule 175 that some words "decidedly more significant" than the first might be used as entry words. One suspects that a similar unnecessary preoccupation with the classificatory implications of formal grammar prevented Cutter from exploiting sub-headings to distinguish those "indistinct" and unestablished subjects which Rule 106 leaves under the names of their nearest class terms.

Cutter's reservation ordering entry under the more significant word is the essential clue to component order in compound subjects. The first word of a phrase is often suited for the role of entry word in a subject heading, not because it 'limits' the following word in the phrase, but because it is the more significant of the two. In order to reach a practically useful rule, we need to clarify the idea of significance, but before attempting this, we must consider three later approaches to the problem.

## NOTES AND REFERENCES

[1] Cutter, C. A. *Rules for a dictionary catalog*, 4th ed. (Washington, 1904).

[2] Pettee, J. *Subject headings* (New York, 1946), p. 80.

[3] Cutter, C. A. *Rules for a dictionary catalog*, p. 72.

[4] Ibid. pp. 74–75.

# CHAPTER V

# SUBJECT HEADING THEORY AFTER CUTTER

## J. KAISER

SINCE the publication of *Rules for a Dictionary Catalog* three attempts have been made to get to closer grips with the problem of the relative significance of the various components of a compound subject. The first is associated with the name of J. Kaiser, Librarian successively of the Philadelphia Commercial Museum and the Tariff Commission, London. Kaiser's approach was essentially concerned with the extraction of detailed pieces of information from a heterogeneous collection of documents. In his own day this seemed more relevant to general business office practice than to libraries, as their functions were then understood, and Kaiser himself contrasted the functions of an index for retrieving information with that of the public library catalogue. The concept of a library as an information store was still some distance in the future. At first sight Kaiser's thought might seem to be of practical relevance to the special librarian alone, and perhaps even then only to the commercial librarian. Again and again he emphasises that subject indexing policy must be entirely guided by the purpose for which the collection of documents has been formed. General public libraries have no purpose definable in terms of the subjects included in their stocks, but Kaiser's system, as one of the very few attempts to consider basic problems in contrast to *ad hoc* difficulties in subject cataloguing, is of practical import to libraries of all kinds.

In his *Systematic Indexing*[1] published in 1911, he lays down the rule that all subjects should be broken down into what he calls a Concrete, followed by a Process. Concretes include things, places, and abstract terms not signifying actions or processes. To the objection that a document can deal with all aspects of a thing, and not only a particular process associated with it, the explanation may be made that 'Description' is included among the Process terms. Process can in fact mean (a) mode of treatment of the subject by the writer, and (b) an action or process described in the document. It can also include (c) an adjective related to the Concrete as complement to subject, e.g.

SAILING VESSELS – Available

Kaiser also makes the point that most Process words imply an object
or material which is the Concrete. Thus a document simply on
'Painting' would conceivably be entered by Kaiser as

PAINT – Application

However this analysis is not made when the Process is associated with a
particular object, as in 'Painting of Boats', which would be entered as

BOATS – Painting

The Concrete element of a compound is the entry word in all cases. A
Concrete need not necessarily be a single word. Adjectival phrases, and
double noun phrases are included. They are always cited as they stand
without inversion. The inclusion of a category of abstract terms as
Concretes gives rise to some uncertainty of definition. Kaiser includes
as Concretes the intangible economic commodities, such as Labour. It
is, on the other hand, not hard to imagine such compounds as 'Children,
Labour', where labour clearly forms the Process element. Where two
Concretes are involved, as Paint and Boat in the example quoted, one
is where possible concealed in the Process word (e.g. as Paint is concealed in the Process-term Painting). Where this is not possible, double
entry is made consisting of each Concrete in association with the same
Process term.

All locality-topic combinations have double entry, the two entries
consisting of

CONCRETE, Place, Process       and
PLACE, Concrete, Process

For example French wine exports would yield two entries:

WINE – France – Export       and
FRANCE – Wine – Export

All local units within a country are cited as dependent subheadings of
the Country term. Relations between countries, like relations between
things which cannot be expressed with the help of a Process term, are
given double entry. No cross references are made from the Process
terms, but every Concrete term has a series of references, to both
hierarchical superiors and inferiors. Thus 'Railways' will include
references both to 'Transport' and to 'Rolling Stock'. The number of
these references may well exceed the number of actual entries, but this
is not necessarily a defect of the system. The approach to the second
and subsequent words of phrases used as Concretes is usually made
through the system of hierarchical references. Thus 'Internal Combustion Engines', would undoubtedly be noticed in the list of references at 'Engines', and probably also at 'Combustion'.

Although Kaiser left a number of matters unresolved,[2] there is little doubt that his contribution to the advance of subject cataloguing technique has been of great importance. He took up the problem of the relative importance of the components of a compound subject at the point at which Cutter had left it. His solution – the division of all terms into two great classes, Concretes, and Processes, according to their meanings – is still a fundamental theorem in subject cataloguing, though it does not provide the answer to all problems. In particular it should be noticed that the distinction between the two classes was not absolutely precise owing to Kaiser's admission of 'abstract Concretes', some of which, like 'Labour', already quoted, have the character of Concretes in some contexts and Processes in others. On the whole, however, Kaiser attempted to derive a subject heading order from the character of individual terms in isolation, rather than from their mutual relationship in the phrase. Compounds comprising more than one Concrete, or Concrete and Property terms were handled by recourse to the somewhat hazardous forms of natural language. As an example may be noted

HIGH TENSION UNDERGROUND ELECTRIC TRACTION
    MOTOR

which might equally well have been rendered in natural language as 'High Tension Electric Underground Traction Motor' or 'Underground Traction High Tension Electric Motor'. No directions for subject cataloguing and indexing can be considered adequate if they do not help the cataloguer to regularise such situations as this. It is to be noted that in Kaiser's straightforward Concrete and Process compounds such as 'BOOKS – Illustration', the subject is actually the interaction between Books and Illustration. In the example of the Underground Traction Motor, the subject is clearly the electric motor and not the interaction between the motor and traction and underground tunnels. The relationship is merely referred to in order to specify a particular kind of electric motor. We shall find later that any combination of terms in an index may mean either the interaction between the things represented by the two terms, or it may mean a particular kind of one of the things, the kind being signalled by the second term. Thus, 'Aircraft, Gas Turbine' may be about the operation and use of the turbine in the aircraft, or it may be about the whole class of aircraft which are propelled by Gas turbines. Kaiser's Concrete and Process formula applied only to compounds with the first type of meaning, which he would perhaps have rendered

AIRCRAFT – Gas turbine propulsion.

For the second type Kaiser would have relied on natural language order to index 'GAS TURBINE AIRCRAFT'. This may be a reasonable expedient here, but as the earlier example of the underground traction motor showed, natural language order can be indeterminate. It is also questionable whether even the alphabetical subject catalogue should not assemble together word combinations composed of the same units.

We may before leaving Kaiser mention three further points on which he was well in advance of his time. The first, which was incorporated as an integral part of his system, was his understanding of the need for references from the specific to the general subject. Although this is the route by which any systematic search for specific information must proceed, its existence is still almost completely unrecognised in dictionary catalogue practice. The other two points are only found in a germinal state in Kaiser's work. He was content to explain or demonstrate them without following them up.

The habit of seeking out the Concrete and Process elements in every subject led Kaiser to the discovery that many apparently simple terms representing Concretes are capable of further breaking down into their logical elements. Thus, as he pointed out, 'Wages' is equivalent to 'LABOUR – Price'. But this opened out highly inconvenient possibilities for a system based upon the simple dual division of terms into Concretes and Processes, for if followed out, it would give for instance 'LABOUR – Price – Increase' instead of the more familiar pattern of 'WAGES – Increase'. The Kaiser system always requires the maximum verbal telescoping of a complex idea, into a single word if possible, otherwise into a phrase, always provided that the telescoping does not lead to a solitary Process-term. At any rate, having mooted the idea, Kaiser drew back, and we find it little applied in his scheme except for the breaking down of Process terms.

Semantic analysis of this kind has the property of exposing relationships in alphabetical sequence. Thus the closely related complex terms 'Wages' and 'Strikes', when arranged in alphabetical sequence, give no hint of the relationship. Broken down into their elementary terms, the two subjects are brought together in alphabetical sequence as

LABOUR – Price
LABOUR – Withdrawal

Unfortunately, enquirers do not habitually think in elementary terms, and like all other devices for grouping related subjects in the alphabetical subject catalogue, it is employed at the cost of a loss of first-reference access to required subjects. For forms of catalogue which deliberately sacrifice first-reference access, such as the classified catalogue and the mechanical selector, semantic analysis offers itself as a tool for future development.

The second germinal point which emerges from Kaiser's book (in particular from his illustrated plates) is that the order in which the sub-headings are arranged when they occur in compounds, is the reverse of the order in which they are arranged in sequence when they occur separately. Thus, if the following heading is correct

    BELGIUM, Liège – Metal – Manufactures

entries for material dealing separately with Liège, Metals of Belgium, and Manufactures of Belgium, are arranged as follows:

    BELGIUM             – Manufactures
    BELGIUM             – Metal
    BELGIUM, Liège       – Description

There is a striking parallel here with a similar phenomenon in the Colon classification, where the order in which components of the class symbol are combined is the reverse of the order in which those same symbols are arranged in the catalogue or shelf sequence when they represent separate subjects. This phenomenon is of some relevance to an alphabetical subject catalogue which contains locality and form subheadings as well as subject subheadings. These are often arranged in separate sequences. Miss Pettee devotes space in her book *Subject Headings*[3] to discussing on an *ad hoc* basis just such problems as whether to give place or form as subheading, or if both in what order. Most of these problems could have been resolved simply by considering how the respective blocks of form and locality entries are ordered in the catalogue with regard to one another. The truth is that both Kaiser, with his separated sequences of sub-localities, Concretes and Processes, and Miss Pettee with her distinct blocks of form, time, and place subheadings, have introduced classificatory order into the dictionary arrangement. This classificatory order is the reverse of the order in which terms from the various blocks are combined together as parts of a compound heading.

### S. R. RANGANATHAN

A more elaborate attempt to fit all terms into a set of categories arranged in order of importance has been made by S. R. Ranganathan, primarily as a basis for constructing the Colon Classification scheme. The classification structure derived from these categories or 'facets' was, in addition, to be the basis for the order of component terms both

in dictionary catalogue subject headings and in classified catalogue subject index entries. A detailed account of Ranganathan's method of
constructing a subject index to the classified catalogue is given in a
later chapter. The present discussion is concerned with two attempts,
one by Ranganathan himself, and the other by A. Thompson, to
utilise the facet formula as a basis for ordering the parts of a compound
heading in an alphabetical subject catalogue.

The notion of 'facets' in classification schedules is by now fairly
widely understood. A schedule for Metal Manufactures would include
on the one hand a list of products, such as bars, plates, tubes, cylindrical
sections, sheets, and so forth, and on the other hand a list of processes
such as casting, welding, pressing, extruding, machining, coating.
Each of these two lists represents a particular exclusive mental angle on
the topic Metal manufactures, and are therefore called 'facets': 'aspects'
would have done just as well. Ranganathan has isolated the facets,
which he has called Personality, Matter, Energy, Space and Time.[4]
These pervade all fields of knowledge and while all five may not
apply to every subject, most subjects have proved to be susceptible to
analysis into four of the categories. From the practical point of view
the order Personality, Matter, Energy, Space, Time is of the utmost
importance, for this is the order in which the constituent parts of the
Colon classification symbol are cited, and of course, it goes without
saying that this order of citation determines where the subject is placed
in the classified sequence. In his *Dictionary Catalogue Code* Ranganathan
uses this facet formula as a basis for the construction of compound
headings for the dictionary catalogue. The order for this purpose is
broadly Energy, Matter, Personality, Space, Time. However, Energy
(in the form of a main class caption or as one of the common subdivisions of the Colon scheme) can occur after Personality, and Space,
or Locality, becomes the Personality facet in certain main classes. The
extended facet formula for dictionary catalogue subject headings is:

Energy, Matter, Personality, Energy (main class heading), Space, Time.

The position of Energy terms represented by common subdivisions
is variable vis-à-vis Space and Time.

A simple example will show how the technique works. The subject
'Harvesting of Grapes' is represented in the classification notation by a
combination of two symbols meaning 'Harvesting' and 'Grapes' respectively. From the facet formula *for class number construction* these
symbols are arranged in the order

Grapes (Personality)      Harvesting (Energy)

The facet formula *for dictionary catalogue subject heading construction* involving in this case Energy and Personality, gives the heading

HARVESTING, Grapes    (ENERGY, Personality)

In the recent 4th edition of the *Classified Catalogue Code*, Ranganathan has considerably extended and refined his original rules for dictionary catalogue headings, partly as a result of new developments in the Colon Classification itself. Though fresh provisions are made for complex class symbols, the basic order of components in the heading appears to be unchanged.

There can be little doubt that Ranganathan's five categories of terms, despite the qualifications and modifications which must be taken into account in any attempt to apply them practically, are a useful improvement on Kaiser's pair. It is unfortunate that the term 'Personality' remains incapable of close definition. It is often equivalent to Kaiser's 'Concrete', but it can also denote function, use, or product.

Some of the difficulties of treating Ranganathan's facets as categories for determining the order of components of subject headings disappear when the total field covered by the catalogue or index is limited. A. Thompson, when Librarian of the Royal Institute of British Architects, found that the Ranganathan facets formed an acceptable basis for component-order in compound headings in an alphabetical subject catalogue.[5] Mr. Thompson did not, however, adopt the order of citation used by Ranganathan. Parts of Buildings common to all kinds of buildings (such as 'Roofs') are given precedence over Personality (which in this context means 'kind of building' – church, hospital, library, and so on). In this catalogue are to be found such headings as

ROOFS, Churches, Renovation
AERODROMES, Runways, Concrete

Installations (Heating, Lighting, Air conditioning) are regarded as Parts of buildings and have priority, giving headings such as

AIR-CONDITIONING: parliament buildings

Compounds of more than four components are not used in this catalogue: where necessary the Material and/or Energy elements are removed leaving Part, Personality, Space, and Time in that order.

### J. E. L. FARRADANE

The basis of Kaiser's scheme and of that devised from Ranganathan's 'facets' is the classification of isolated terms into categories. There is a given order of precedence of these categories: so that to arrive at a subject heading we have merely to assign each component to its category, and then rearrange in category order.[6]

An alternative approach to compound subject headings is to consider not the component terms themselves but the relationships between each pair of them. It can be argued that categories such as Kaiser's or Ranganathan's are comparatively superficial manifestations of modes of relationship between pairs of terms. Thus, the categorisation

(Concrete) Grape      (Process) Harvesting

might be described simply as an 'action' relationship between two concepts without reference to any attributes of the two concepts themselves, such as concreteness or abstractness. Similarly, the ordered categories

(Concrete) Bank      (Process) Lending

might be treated as an instance of 'causation' relationship.

An approach to classification and subject indexing has been made along these lines by J. E. L. Farradane,[7] who distinguishes nine kinds of relationships governing the way in which terms are placed together. Terms and their relationships are more precisely defined in Science and Technology than elsewhere, and it is in this field that Farradane's relational analysis has its most obvious sphere of application. The same basic methods are, however, believed to be valid for the Social Sciences and Humanities.

The nine relationships are derived ultimately from the account of the learning process given by the psychologists W. E. Vinacke, N. Isaacs, and G. R. Miller. Farradane draws attention to the two qualities of experience which act together to determine our sense of variety in the way concepts are related. These two qualities are the time sense and awareness of degrees of distinctness in the possible ways in which concepts may be related. Three degrees of each of the two qualities are recognised. The first may be non-time, temporary or fixed: the second may be merely concurrent, non-distinct or distinct. The six possible qualities may be combined to give nine pairs which correspond to the nine possible relationships.

In concurrent relationships the two concepts are merely together in an undefined situation which constitutes the link between them. In non-distinct relationship the two concepts are directly attached to one another, though the precise mode of attachment is not known or given. In the case of distinct relationship, the connection between the two concepts is clear and explicit.

Examining each of these three in conjunction with the three time sense qualities, we find that the distinct-fixed (or permanent) relation amounts to *Causation* or *Functional Dependence*; the distinct-temporary relation is *Action upon*; and the distinct-non-time relation is *Distinction from, Substitution for,* or *Imitation*. Turning now to the triad of non-distinct relations, we find that non-distinct-permanent yields the idea of *Belonging to*, as for instance, a physical property belonging to a substance. This relationship is often represented in language by the genitive construction. Non-distinct-temporary gives what Farradane calls the *Dimensional* relation, which includes spatial, temporal and other properties derived by an object from its environment. The non-distinct-non-time relation is simply *Equivalence* to some degree, or the relation between synonyms. Of the three concurrent relationships, the combination concurrent-permanent gives *Association*. The linguistic signpost for this relation is the preposition 'for'; it also comprehends subjective properties, as for instance, the Sombreness of Anglo-Saxon verse. The concurrent-temporary relation covers *Comparison* and the relation between *Agent and Activity*, as for instance, Bird migration. Finally, concurrence-non-time relationship means simply the *Co-presence* in the mind of two concepts otherwise unrelated.

The following examples illustrate the use of some of the nine relationships described above:

1   Signing a will in the presence of witnesses
    Will (action) Signing (co-presence) Witnesses

2   Use of classification in searching scientific literature
    Science (association) Literature (action) Searching (association) Classification

3   A depression bringing rain to the British Isles
    Depression (causation) Rain (dimension) British Isles

4   Prevention of bacterial infection following the grafting of trees
    Trees (action) Grafting (association) Infection (association) Bacteria (action) Prevention

5   Soil friability affecting ploughing
    Ploughing (action) Soil (belonging) Friability

Farradane employs a notation to indicate the nine relations, each of which is represented by a sign consisting of two parts, known as an 'operator'. The order of the parts indicates the direction of the relationship.

Expressed in operator notation, the examples given above now appear as follows:

1   Will /– Signing Ø Witnesses
2   Science /; Literature /– Searching /; Classification
3   Depression /: Rain /+ British Isles
4   Trees /– Grafting /; Infection [/; Bacteria] /– Prevention
5   Ploughing /– Soil /( Friability

Approximate and non-comprehensive meanings of the operators used above are:

/:  causes or produces
/–  is the object of action by
/(  includes or contains
/+  has the environment-property of
/;  is associated with
Ø   in the presence of

The compounds can be reversed, if required, provided that the operators are quoted in reversed form. For example:

1   Witnesses Ø Signing –/ Will
2   Classification ;/ Searching –/ Literature ;/ Science
3   British Isles +/ Rain :/ Depression
4   Prevention –/ [Bacteria ;/] Infection ;/ Grafting –/ Trees
5   Friability )/ Soil –/ Ploughing

The brackets in example No. 4 are required because infection is directly related to each of the three concepts Trees, Bacteria, and Prevention. A linear sequence can signify only two relationships on either side of the concept, so the brackets are needed as an auxiliary device. In the example they indicate an insertion into the otherwise properly articulated pair Prevention –/ Infection. Other permutations, designed to bring a particular term into a leading position, can be achieved by the use of brackets. Thus, it would be possible to have

Literature [;/ Science] /– Searching /; Classification.

It should be noted that this device does not permit complete permutation. We cannot have two pairs of brackets next to one another.

The actual order of components chosen for alphabetical indexing will depend upon the known point of view of the majority of the users of a particular library. The system thus offers no rule for component order in a neutral subject catalogue. It does, however, once the desired component has been chosen as entry word, prescribe logical limits on the way in which the remaining terms may be arranged. It is of interest, and perhaps not without relevance to the problem of the neutral subject catalogue, that Farradane does lay down a definite arrangement of components when the system is used to construct a classification scheme. This is the order produced when the operators have the /

before the relation sign, and brackets are eliminated or reduced to a minimum. This preferred deductive order corresponds to the time order between components, but is the reverse of the order which we use when we define the compound in natural language. Thus, to take one of the examples just discussed, in point of time-relationship Science precedes its Literature, which precedes Searching, which precedes Classification. On the other hand the natural linguistic order is 'Classification as method of Search of Literature of Science'.

Farradane's study of relationships has thrown into relief several points of possible relevance to the formulation of rules for compound subject headings in neutral catalogues. In the first place at the level of language, relationships are verbs, linking noun-concepts into pairs. In the ordinary usage of language, the relational verb often disappears leaving a preposition as its representative. Thus 'of' implies 'belongs to'. For most kinds of relationships, there is an unequal emphasis on the connected concepts. Or in other words, relationship is not a meeting of two concepts at a mid-point rendezvous but a carrying over of one concept, which is, as it were, moveable for the occasion to another concept which is fixed. Thus in the expression 'Divine right of Kings' it is the idea of divine sanction which is carried over or applied to kings, and not vice versa. 'Kings' is the fixed component in the compound, and often the most heavily stressed syllable in the spoken phrase. The string of components forming the compound may be in simple linear relationship, as A relates to B, B relates to C, etc., or the relationships may be multidirectional, as A relates to B, B relates to C, B relates to D, in which case we have to contemplate the possibility that our subject may contain contiguous components, such as C and D in this example, not directly related to one another.

## NOTES AND REFERENCES

[1] Kaiser, J. *Systematic indexing* (London, 1911).

[2] See Vickery, B. C. *Structure of a connective index.* J. Docum. Vol. 6, 1950, pp. 140–151.

[3] Pettee, J. *Subject headings* (New York, 1946), pp. 127, 147.

[4] See Palmer, B. I. & Wells, A. J. *Fundamentals of library classification* (London, 1951).

[5] Thompson, A. *Rules for subject headings.* J. Docum. Vol. 9, 1953, pp. 169–174.

[6] See also Vickery, B. C. *Classification and indexing in science.* 2nd ed. (London, 1959), pp. 31–36.

[7] Farradane, J. E. L. *A scientific theory of classification and indexing.* J. Docum. Vol. 6, 1950, pp. 83–99 and Vol. 8, 1952, pp. 73–92.

# Chapter VI

# SIGNIFICANCE AND TERM RELATIONSHIP
# IN COMPOUND HEADINGS

Of the three attempts described in the last chapter to resolve the question of word order in compound subject headings, the first two – those of Kaiser and Ranganathan – are developments of Cutter's idea of 'significance' as a special property of particular words in isolation. Farradane's approach to the problem is the exact reverse of this: he scrutinises, not the component words themselves, but the relationships between them.

In this chapter some further problems of component order in headings are considered, both by way of the meanings of the respective components and of the relationships between them. We shall find that over a wide area both approaches yield the same result. Over a more limited range of problems one or other of the two approaches may be unhelpful, but it is only rarely that neither can contribute to a solution.

### TERM SIGNIFICANCE

The most significant term in a compound is the one which is most readily available to the memory of the enquirer. This, in turn, is the word which evokes the clearest mental image.

Modern science accustoms us to the view that everything in the universe is a manifestation of energy. However acceptable this may be intellectually, everyone in practice makes an imaginative distinction between 'things' and 'actions'. This applies even to the physicist. He still finds it necessary to think of 'particles' side by side with the purely dynamic concept of wave motion. Etymologically a 'thing' is whatever one can think, that is to say whatever can be thought of as a static image. In this special sense it includes not only the names of physical objects but systems and organisations of a mental kind. Images of things are simpler, more readily formed, more accessible to memory than images of actions because time does not enter into them. We can, for instance, visualise a cat, and we can return to the same image again and again. If, however, we try to imagine the cat in action, let us say springing, we need a series of visual 'stills'; the cat all bunched up at the ready, the cat in mid-leap in the air, the cat landing, and so on.

Now if we remove the cat, leaving only the notion 'springing', what is there left to imagine? Perhaps only the vague trajectory of anything that rises from the ground and then falls, a curving line in fact. This is the best that the visual imagination can do to turn an action into a 'thing' and even this, it may be noted, is only made possible by eliminating the time element. The trajectory line represents beginning, middle and end of the action as being all present at once.

The enquirer's choice as to which word-component of a compound subject he will try first in the catalogue or index, will fall on that word which gives the most definite image. Assuming that he knows that he wants the 'Springing of Cats', he will begin by looking up 'Cat' rather than 'Springing', because 'Cat' produces a more definite image in his mind than 'Springing'. 'Cat' is in fact the more significant word.

With reservations to be detailed later, we can say that a word which evokes a static image is more significant than one which denotes actions or processes. A static image is produced by names of 'things' and names of materials. The difference between the two from the point of view of the imagination is that a 'thing' has a boundary, while a material has none. For this reason we must rate the name of a material lower in significance than the name of a 'thing'. On the other hand, the image of a material is made up of entirely static-seeming properties such as colour, hardness, smoothness, so we must rate it higher in significance than the name of an action.

Thus far the following order of significance has been set up:

Thing/Material/Action.

## TERM RELATIONSHIPS

This represents the limit to which we can go in elucidating the order of component words from a consideration of their meanings and the images they invoke. While the significance order is fundamental in indexing and subject cataloguing, it does not alone answer all questions of component order. Compound subjects may include two or more equally concrete things, and we find that natural language sometimes may use the same pair of components in reversed order to convey two distinct ideas: thus 'Conveyor belt' and 'Belt conveyor'. It is clear that significance order and natural language order cannot be reconciled in all cases. The relationship between the members of each pair is not the same. 'Conveyor belt' is equivalent to Belt of Conveyor, that is Belt as part of a Conveyor, while 'Belt conveyor' denotes a kind of Conveyor, namely that which includes a Belt. The same two words, however, jostle one another in the mind of the enquirer preparing to consult the catalogue, irrespective of whether the subject of his search is 'Conveyor belt' or 'Belt conveyor'.

In order to decide issues of this kind, and many apparently simpler ones, it is necessary to consider (1) how far relationships between components lead to modifications of the significance formula Thing / Material / Action and (2) how far the significance formula leads to the modification of the natural language order of the word-components.

One way of approaching the question of relationship between the word-components is to consider how relationship is rendered in natural language.[1] The simpler relationships between concepts are expressed, and to a great extent differentiated, by prepositions. Amplified to prepositional phrases, our two examples above become 'Belt of conveyor' and 'Conveyor with belt' respectively. The 'of' and 'with' indicate how the component words are related. Most compound phrases consisting of two nouns can be easily amplified in this way to clarify the kind of relationship between components. The same can be said of most adjective-noun phrases, where we simply substitute the noun equivalent of the adjective in the amplified prepositional phrase. Thus 'Social psychology', on amplification, becomes 'Psychology of society'. It should be noticed, too, that the normal way of naming or defining a new concept is to take two established names and connect them by means of a preposition, e.g. 'Intelligence of cephalopods'. This is of some importance, as it suggests the possibility of a unified approach not only to compound subject phrases but also to those 'unestablished' compounds to which Cutter was content to give class entry only.

The simplest of all relationships between concepts is represented by the genitive 'of'. For subject heading purposes, we reverse the order of the concepts from that in which they stand in the amplified prepositional phrase. In other words, the last term (or sometimes its adjectival equivalent) in the prepositional phrase becomes the entry-word in the subject heading. Thus 'Exploitation of invertebrates' becomes 'INVERTEBRATES, Exploitation' in the subject heading, while 'Deterioration of oil transformers' becomes 'TRANSFORMERS, Oil, Deterioration'. It will be noticed that the subject headings in both cases are in accordance with the significance order: in the first case Thing / Action, in the second Thing / Material / Action. However, the discovery that where the connecting preposition is 'of' the subject heading order of components is the reverse of their order in the prepositional phrase, enables us to go beyond the significance formula in determining the order of many compounds consisting of two 'things'. 'Conveyor belt' amplifies to 'Belt of conveyor', and is therefore entered as it stands in natural language. We can say that a word signifying a part of a Thing follows the word denoting the whole Thing in compound subject headings. A word denoting property follows in the subject the name of the Thing, Material or Action to which it applies. For example, 'Fastness of dyes and Stability of flight' yield the subject headings 'DYES, Fastness', and 'FLIGHT, Stability'. So far all kinds of phrases with the connecting word 'of' have given rise to subject headings which reverse the order of components. There is an exception to this where 'of' is equivalent to 'made of' and connects the name of a Thing to the name of a Material. Here the order of subject heading components is the same as that of the prepositional phrase. Thus 'Bricks of glass' becomes merely 'BRICKS, Glass'. This exceptional situation is due to the effect of significance order which in this instance insists on retaining the order Thing / Material. It should be observed that the subject heading 'BRICKS, Glass' could mean either Glass Bricks or the Glass used as Brick material. This ambiguity occurs wherever the effect of the significance order upsets the normal reversed relationship between prepositional phrase and subject heading. The distinction can be made clear in practice either by different punctuation for the first case, or by saying 'BRICKS, Glass type' or 'BRICKS, Glass of'.

Passing now to the relational word 'for', the first point to be made is that any compound which might equally well be rendered in the amplified form with 'of' or 'for' should be treated according to the rules given for the former. 'For', in its most common usage, implies a relationship, not very dissimilar from that denoted by the preposition 'of'. FOOD in the two phrases 'Preservation of food' and 'Container for food' is the object of an action in the first case and of an implied action in the second case, and is the entry word in both cases. When the names of two things are connected by 'for', the first, if not actually a part o the second, serves or contributes to it. What is served or contributed to becomes the entry word. As with the preposition 'of', the subject heading reverses the order of the names in the prepositional phrase. In all such phrases there is the implicit idea that the first 'thing' could apply or contribute to a number of other things though it is only being applied to one in this particular instance. Thus in 'Telescopes for astronomy' and 'Libraries for the public' (subject heading forms 'ASTRONOMY, Telescopes', and 'PUBLIC LIBRARIES'), Astronomy and the Public are each only one of a number of fields of application for Telescopes and Libraries. It is to be noted from the examples of 'FOOD, Containers' and 'ASTRONOMY, Telescopes', that compounds, based on the 'for' relationship do not necessarily produce subject headings corresponding to the significance formula. Care should be taken not to confuse the 'for' relationship so far considered, with the special use of 'for' in natural language to distinguish homonyms. For instance, we have 'Counter' as an item of shop or office equipment, and 'Counter' meaning a coloured disc used in some board games and tiddly-winks. We might reasonably express the difference as 'Counters for business premises' and 'Counters for games'. The subject heading in this case follows the order of the prepositional phrase: 'COUNTERS, Business equipment', and 'COUNTERS, Games'. A similar caution may be extended to the pedagogical-literary relationship implied in 'Physics for engineers' or 'Social science for nurses'. This is Ranganathan's bias phase. The subject headings in such cases are identical with the prepositional phrases.

Phrases which include 'for' followed by the gerund, reverse the order of names for subject headings, if the gerund expresses purpose. If the gerund merely expresses a method of operation, the subject heading components follow the order of the prepositional phrase. Two examples will make this clear. In 'Machine for washing', the gerund gives the function or purpose of the machine, and the subject heading is in the reverse order 'Washing machine'. In 'Library for lending', the gerund states how the library carries out its function of making literary and other library material available to library users. 'Lending' refers to a method of operation and not to the ultimate function of the library.

Phrases which on amplification exhibit the relational word 'against' yield a compound subject heading with the components reversing the order of the amplified phrase. They may not always coincide with the significance formula. Natural language may differentiate a particular kind of Thing, by referring to the fact that it includes a special part, is made of a special material, or works by a special principle of action. We have already noticed the case in which kind is designated by material in the example of 'Bricks of glass', and in that case it was observed that the significance formula led to the citation of the differentiating 'Glass' as a subheading of the Thing 'Brick'. A similar reversal of natural language order for subject heading purposes occurs when a part is quoted to designate a particular kind of Thing. The relational word in this case is 'with', such as occurs in the phrase 'Bridge with girder', for which the subject heading form is 'BRIDGE, Girder'. The transposition of the natural language form 'Girder bridge' is to be attributed in this instance not to the significance formula, but to the effect of the fundamental Whole-Part relationship between the components, which though not actually in question in the phrase demands

# RELATIONSHIP TABLE

| Type of compound | Subject Heading Order | Subject Heading agrees or reverses significance order | Subject Heading agrees or reverses amplified phrase order | Usual relationship words in amplified phrase |
|---|---|---|---|---|
| 1 Action on Thing | THING, Action | Agrees | Reverses | of |
| 2 Action on Material | MATERIAL, Action | Agrees | Reverses | of |
| 3 Action A on Action B | Action B, Action A | — | Reverses | of, in |
| 4 Material of Thing | THING, Material | Agrees | Reverses | of |
| 5 Part of Thing | THING, Part | — | Reverses | of |
| 6 Property of Thing, Material or Action | THING MATERIAL ACTION } Property | Agrees | Reverses | of |
| 7 Partial viewpoint on Thing, Material or Action, or Property | THING MATERIAL ACTION PROPERTY } Viewpoint | — | Reverses | of |
| 8 Thing *distinguished* by citation of Principle of Action | THING, Action | Agrees | Agrees | with based on |
| 9 Thing *distinguished* by citation of Material | THING, Material | Agrees | Agrees | of |
| 10 Thing *distinguished* by citation of Part | THING, Part | Agrees | Agrees | with |
| 11 Thing *distinguished* by Material or Form of energy which it utilises | MATERIAL FORM OF ENERGY } Thing | Reverses | Reverses | operated by |
| 12 Action A *distinguished* by citation of contributory or underlying Action B | ACTION A, Action B | — | Agrees | by |
| 13 Thing A, *serving, supplying or aiming* at Thing B | THING B, Thing A | — | Reverses | for serving as |
| 14 Thing A or Action A *distinguished* from a homonym by the fact that it *serves* Thing B or Action B | THING A, Thing B<br>THING A, Action B<br>ACTION A, Action B | —<br>Agrees<br>— | Agrees<br>Agrees<br>Agrees | for |
| 15 Thing *serving or instrumental* to Action | ACTION, Thing | Reverses | Reverses | for |
| 16 Thing A *caused* by Thing B | THING B, Thing A | — | Reverses | caused by produced by devised by |
| 17 Thing *caused* by Action | THING, Action | Agrees | Agrees | caused by produced by |
| 18 Action *caused* by Thing | THING, Action | Agrees | Reverses | of caused by |
| 19 Action A *caused* by Action B | ACTION A, Action B | — | Agrees | caused by |
| 20 Thing or Action at a type of location | LOCATION, Thing<br>LOCATION, Action | —<br>Agrees | Reverses<br>Reverses | at, of<br>at, of |

the continued use of Whole/Part order. 'With' may also govern a word denoting a special principle of action, as in the example 'Gear utilising friction'. This relational phrase order is retained in the subject heading 'GEAR, Friction (Type)', which is also in accordance with the Thing/Action order of the significance formula. It is important to bear in mind the distinction between action-word denoting principle of operation and action-word designating function or purpose. In the latter case the relation is given by the word 'for' and the subject heading, contrary to the significance-formula, is in the form Action/ Thing. Occasionally compounds occur which comprise the name of a thing coupled with that of a material, which the Thing consumes in operation. 'Gas turbine', and 'Steam engine' are examples. Such combinations should receive a subject heading in the form Material/Thing, which reverses both amplified phrase order, and significance order.

Kinds of Things and kinds of Actions are often specified in natural language by reference to causative or initiating factors. On amplification such compounds yield phrases containing the preposition 'by'. Where the components are Thing and Action, they are cited in that order, in accordance with the significance formula. Where they are both Actions, the Action which is caused or initiated becomes the entry word of the subject heading. 'BANKS, Lending' (i.e. Lending by banks) is a subject heading of the first type, where the components are Thing and Action. 'HEATING, Induction' (i.e. Heating caused by induction) is an example of the second type in which both components are terms denoting Action.

The Relationship Table opposite details the types of compounds discussed here, with their subject heading forms in connection with the significance formula and the order of components in the corresponding amplified phrase.

The table overleaf with its twenty categories of compounds may at first sight seem too formidably complicated to serve as a basis for the practical construction of subject headings. A closer inspection of the table shows however that the only details the cataloguer is called upon to memorise are groups of exceptions to the rule that the order of components in the subject heading is the reverse of their order in the amplified relational phrase. The exceptions are (a) where 'for' is used to distinguish homonyms (No. 14 in table), (b) where a Part, Material, or method of Action is quoted to differentiate a particular kind of Thing (Nos. 8, 9, 10 in table), (c) where a particular Action is distinguished by citing a subordinate Action which contributes to it (No. 12 in table), (d) where the relation is that of causation.

The following examples of compound subjects illustrate the types of combination enumerated in the table.

| Type No. | Amplified phrase | Subject Heading |
|---|---|---|
| 1 | Driving of piles<br>Planning of villages | PILES, Driving<br>VILLAGES, Planning |
| 2 | Casting of aluminium<br>Fitting of gas (equipment) | ALUMINIUM, Casting<br>GAS, Fitting |
| 3 | Corruption in politics | POLITICS, Corruption |
| 4 | Wood of roofs | ROOFS, Wood |
| 5 | Wheel of bicycle | BICYCLES, Wheels |
| 6 | Fertility of rodents<br>Strength of concrete<br>Speed of corrosion | RODENTS, Fertility<br>CONCRETE, Strength<br>CORROSION, Speed |
| 7 | Theory of structures<br>Physics of metals<br>Ethics of hunting | STRUCTURES, Theory<br>METALS, Physics<br>HUNTING, Ethics |
| 8 | Bridges based on suspension (principle) | BRIDGES, Suspension (type) |
| 9 | Rectifiers made of selenium | RECTIFIERS, Selenium (type) |
| 10 | Books with illustrations | BOOKS, Illustrated |
| 11 | Engines operated by steam (pressure)<br>Machinery operated by electricity | STEAM, Engines<br>ELECTRICITY, Machinery |
| 12 | Welding by (exploiting electrical) resistance (properties of metals) | WELDING, Resistance |
| 13 | Transformers for radio (equipment)<br>Trucks for cattle | RADIO, Transformers<br>CATTLE, Trucks |
| 14 | Accelerators for high energy physics<br>Accelerators for composting | ACCELERATORS, High energy Physics<br>ACCELERATORS, Composting |
| 15 | Machines for planing | PLANING, Machines |
| 16 | Craters caused by meteorites | METEORITES, Craters |
| 17 | Crystals produced by condensation | CRYSTALS, Condensation (types) |
| 18 | Phenomena caused by spirits | PSYCHICAL PHENOMENA |
| 19 | Fires caused by lightning | FIRES, Lightning |
| 20 | Plants found in deserts | DESERTS, Plants |

It will be noticed that categories 1–7 in the table are of a totally different character from those numbered 8 to 20. 1 to 7 deal with Properties, Actions, Materials, Viewpoints, and Parts in relation to one another and to Things. Categories 8 to 20 deal, not with Actions, Parts, Materials as such, but with Things, differentiated by reference to Parts, Materials, Principles of Action, Function, Material or Energy consumed, and Causative Factors.

We have already noticed that when we are dealing with Actions, Properties, Materials as such, our subject heading can be represented by the significance formula.

THING, Material, Action.

We can expand this by incorporating the relational category Part, which always follows Thing

THING, Part, Material, Action, Property

We can substitute for Thing any of the pairs given in column 2 of the Table in types 8 to 20, provided that the relationship between the two first elements in the subject heading is in fact that described in column 1 of the Table. We can, for example, have

(Type 8)   THING, Action, Part, Material, Action, Property
(Type 9)   THING, Material, Part, Material, Action, Property
(Type 10)  THING, Part, Part, Material, Action, Property
(Type 11)  MATERIAL, Thing, Part, Material, Action, Property
(Type 13)  THING, Thing, Part, Material, Action
(Type 15)  ACTION, Thing, Part, Material, Action, Property
(Type 16)  THING, Thing, Part, Material, Action, Property
(Type 17)  THING, Action, Part, Material, Action

The following are examples of subject headings derived from the significance formula as thus expanded:

(Type 8)   BRIDGES, Suspension, Cables, Heat treatment
(Type 9)   RECTIFIERS, Selenium, Casing, Size
(Type 10)  BOOKS, Illustrated, Paper, Coating, Density
(Type 11)  STEAM, Engines, Non-ferrous parts, Corrosion
(Type 13)  RADIO, Transformers, Terminals, Metal, Pitting
(Type 14)  ACCELERATORS, Composting, Catalysts, Determination
(Type 15)  PLANING, Machines, Cutters, Grinding
(Type 16)  METEORITES, Craters, Dating

It is believed that the categories of compounds listed in the table cover many of the problems commonly met by cataloguers and indexers. Two fairly obvious omissions are Thing differentiated by a Property not covered by category 8, and Action distinguished by Property. Examples are 'Linear accelerators' and 'First aid'. While the intuitive solutions to the examples quoted ('ACCELERATORS, Linear', and 'FIRST AID') come readily, it would seem that an embracing solution must await more detailed investigation into the possible different kinds of Property. For similar reasons it has not been possible to give a covering rule for the case of Thing acted upon, Action, Agent, though the formula 'THING, Agent, Action' appears often to be suitable. Another variety of compound which sometimes proves troublesome is exemplified by the phrase 'Paper insulated cables'. Here perhaps we can detect a clue in the fact that natural language tends to rid itself of the mediating participle. 'CABLES, Paper' would perhaps be intelligible, but if we prefer not to anticipate terminological development we can enter in the form 'CABLES, Paper insulated'.

The table can be used directly for determining the subject heading form of phrases consisting of two nouns connected by a preposition, or for any subject which requires to be defined or explained by such a phrase, because it has not yet acquired a shorter and more distinct name. Phrases consisting of two nouns (as 'Telephone kiosk') are more usually entered as they stand, than otherwise, but individual cases should be checked by converting into amplified phrase form (i.e. noun-relational word(s)-noun) and checking with the table. Adjective and noun phrases require first that the adjective be turned into its equivalent noun, and that the appropriate phrase linking the two nouns should be found and checked with the table. Thus 'Comparative anatomy' is first changed into 'Comparison, Anatomy', after which the linkage between the two words is expressed by the phrase 'Comparison of anatomies'. On inspection of those categories of the table which have 'of' in the final column of the Relationship Table, this example is seen to be a case of Action upon a Thing, and according to the direction given in the second column the subject heading then becomes 'ANATOMY, Comparative'. A somewhat higher proportion of adjective and noun phrases will prove to require inversion than is the case for double noun phrases.

### PHRASES V. SUBHEADINGS

The last example raises the question as to whether the adjective should be retained as a part of the subject heading or whether it should be turned into substantive form. At one remove is the further question as to whether double noun phrases should be split up, as has generally been done in the examples in this chapter. The basic indexing unit is the single word and any device for focusing the enquirer's attention on the single entry word is likely to be appreciated by him, even if the result is not natural language.

'MOUNTAINS, Birds', is nearly as intelligible as 'Mountain birds', and the representation of all available material on Mountains by the single subsequence under 'MOUNTAINS' is a simpler proposition for the enquirer than a sequence under 'Mountain' used as an adjective, followed by another sequence under 'Mountains'. The idea of assembling everything relating to Mountains under the single word could, of course, be carried further. We could index Mountaineering as 'MOUNTAINS, Climbing'. This was in fact advocated by J. Kaiser, author of *Systematic Indexing*, who attempted to split up all words denoting complex actions into Thing and Action components.[2] As a general rule all double noun phrases are best divided in the form 'MOUNTAINS, Birds'. Adjective-noun phrases are more problematic. 'Nocturnal birds' is certainly better rendered 'NIGHT, Birds', but there seems some disadvantage in turning 'Mental Hygiene' into 'MIND, Hygiene'. Possibly the operative factor here is that in hygiene topics the technical substantives based on the Greek 'psyche' are well established in preference to Mind. Even the Subconscious Mind has now become the Subconscious. Adjectives qualifying nouns denoting Action (as 'First aid') must inevitably be entered without change. There seems no reason why inverted adjectives should not retain adjectival form.

In the preceding sections, the singular or plural forms of terms have been used indifferently, according to which seemed best to illustrate the point being made. We might have less hesitation in separating the components of Mountain Birds if, as the result of adopting the singular form, the result were 'MOUNTAIN, Bird'. The question of double sub-sequences based on 'Mountain' and 'Mountains' respectively no longer arises. No doubt this is one factor which has led S. R. Ranganathan to advocate the singular form in a type of index in which adjectives are, as far as possible, replaced by nouns.[3] The argument for the use of the singular form gains added force in consideration of the fact that English plural forms often produce a complete transformation in the spelling of the last syllable, and the two sub-sequences may be separated by an appreciable body of irrelevant material. On the other hand, a subject heading representing tangible objects normally signals information not on a single specimen of the object, but on the class of those objects. It is therefore natural that we should expect the plural form of heading in catalogues and indexes.

Traditional practice amply confirms this expectation, which is thus heavily fortified by psychological conditioning. If, for the remainder of this book, plural forms are used, it is done as a concession to this conditioning, not out of any conviction that it is necessarily the more practicable alternative. Further enquiry into the character of an optimum index language may well suggest the contrary.

## NAMES OF LOCALITIES IN HEADINGS

It will by now have become clear that what was lacking in Cutter's theory of subject headings was the concept of an artificially modified language for indexing purpose. In the Cutter scheme of things, natural language forms were to suffice. Therefore only subjects which were clear-cut entities in natural language could be expressed, and these same clear-cut entities, if they consisted of word combinations, were to be given in the order of natural language – unless – and here was the visible snag to the dependence on natural language – the decidedly superior significance of a particular word dictated some other order. With that proviso, we have moved outside the sphere of strictly natural language; the present discussion on compound subjects has been an attempt to follow up some of its implications.

Cutter's handling of the locality *v.* topic problem was strictly in accordance with the customs of natural language. In speech, particularly, we tend to give the place-name before the topic name, where necessary turning place-names to adjectival use, in such phrases as 'Surrey Hills' or 'Stockholm Churches'. Cutter faithfully reflects this in his preference for locality as entry word with topic as subheading. Subsequent generations of cataloguers have been compelled to recognise that the problem of significance enters into the locality *v.* topic issue, and Cutter's rule is virtually a dead letter.

In modern practice, entry under topic is preferred in the majority of cases. Most cataloguers agree that there are exceptional cases in which the entry word should be the locality, but there is little consensus as to the actual extent or character of the exceptions. The difficulty is probably that in our apprehension of Place, we waver uncertainly between regarding it as a mere Property of the thing (or action) with which it is associated, and treating it as a Thing in its own right, of which the other component in the compound then becomes a mere Part. Thus 'Cathedrals of France' may be considered as those cathedrals with a particular locality property, known as France, or as a Part of the general entity France. Our thinking when faced with this issue in practical form depends upon the nature of the non-locality component. Subjects, treated in documents with limitation of locality, are not all equally conditioned by the local limitation. Thus, two books respectively on British and German lathe practice are closer together in respect of subject matter than are two books on British and German tax systems. A place-name applied to any subject implies location, and with some subjects the idea of a local community may be more or less strongly implied. Where the idea of a community is most strongly implied, the subject concerned is strongly and significantly conditioned by the locality limitation. We can attempt to rank the main areas of knowledge according to the extent to which they appear to be significantly conditioned by locality:

1 Geography & biological phenomena
2 History & social phenomena
3 Language & literature
4 Fine arts
5 Philosophy & religion
6 Technology
7 Phenomena of physical sciences

The higher a topic appears in this list, the more is its actual subject content likely to be conditioned by locality. At the top of the list, the highest possible local variations exist in local geography, meteorology, flora and fauna. The human communities which take second place in the list exhibit slightly less differentiation in different localities; and of course, language and literature differences are among the most striking products of the differences of the local communities from which they emanate. Local differences are less accentuated in fine arts, because, despite the existence of definite local schools and styles, these arts are not dependent on actual local languages. Similar characteristically local schools of philosophy and religion are to be found, but they are in turn less definite than the schools of artists. In technology the significance of locality is still more slight, while in physical science it may be considered negligible.

Subjects near the top of the list would seem to require entry under the locality-term, with the subject term as subheading. Those at the bottom clearly demand entry under the subject, with locality subheading. The problem is at what point in the middle of the list should the change be made. Conventional modern usage prescribes locality entry for the subject categories (1) to (3) above, but excluding biology.

Library of Congress excludes Fine arts from locality-entry, but nevertheless enters under place some topics belonging to category (5) above.

In the higher categories of the list a further complication is met. For while the broad and collective topics here may be significantly determined by locality, the same may not be true for minute topics included. Thus 'FRANCE, Animals', we may reasonably expect, will refer to something significantly different from, say, 'GREECE, Animals', but if we take a single species, for instance 'FRANCE, Nightingales' and 'GREECE, Nightingales', the difference in what is described in the document may be slight or almost non-existent.

A further possible point of view is that locality-entry should be extended to all fixed objects, both natural, as land forms, trees, etc., and technological, as for instance, roads and buildings. The reasonable ground for this viewpoint is the fact that fixed objects are more closely associated with their localities than moveable ones. The chief difficulty in applying such a rule would be in the fact that each of these objects has closely associated with it an activity, such as Road construction and Building, which would still be entered under the subject term, with locality subheading.

In view of the growth of communications, and the interchange and mixing of ideas and cultures, it seems advisable to limit the categories of subjects which are to be entered under the place-name. It is suggested that as a practical working policy, entry under the place with subject as subheading should be limited to topics in Geography, Geology, History, Social sciences, Linguistics, Literature, Ecology, and the names of groups of natural organisms, plant and animal. Terms denoting study in these fields, such as Historiography, and Literary Criticism should be excluded from this rule, and entered under topic name with locality subheading. Locally-limited topics in Fine arts, Technology, Science, Philosophy and Religion are preferably to be entered under topic name with locality as subheading.

A secondary issue in connection with place names concerns the use of the substantive versus adjectival form. The use of national adjective as entry word is restricted in conventional practice to Linguistics and Literature. As subheading, the local adjective is to be preferred for the designation of local schools of art and philosophy. There is a good case for extending its use as the form of local subheading of scientific and technological subjects. At times its use is obligatory, as for instance in such a heading as 'MOUNTAINEERING, Italian – Switzerland', meaning the exploits of Italian mountaineers on Swiss mountains.

Some components which need to be given in compound headings

may represent concepts which are over-familiar to enquirers. They are taken as understood and not expected to play any part in the index. This issue arises particularly in connection with locality headings and subheadings. The rule that certain social science topics are to be entered under locality works well enough for foreign countries and special towns or districts of Britain, but the British enquirer takes his own country for granted, and does not expect its name to exercise any critical arranging effect in the index. In fact, he is often rather vague as to what this name is. It may be Britain, Great Britain, England (if the enquirer was born south of the Cheviot Hills and east of Offa's Dyke) or the United Kingdom and Northern Ireland. So while 'Italy, Economic planning': 'Mexico, Economic planning': and 'Lancashire, Economic planning' are entered according to the suggested rule, the economic planning of Britain is entered as 'ECONOMIC PLANNING – British', located between material on 'ECONOMIC PLANNING' in general and the first subject subheading. Even where subheadings alone are involved, as in

RAILWAYS
RAILWAYS – Brazilian
RAILWAYS – British
RAILWAYS – Bulgarian

the arrangement is likely to prove disconcerting to British enquirers, and may result in information being overlooked. The remedy is to de-alphabetise the word 'British' by enclosing it in curves or some similar device to which priority arranging value is assigned. This will give the more satisfactory order:

RAILWAYS
RAILWAYS – (British)
RAILWAYS – Brazilian
RAILWAYS – Bulgarian

It is odd that no attempt has been made to frame a rule to cover the subject compound consisting of Place and Event or Period, such as, for instance, Reformation in France. The omission may briefly be made good here. Subject compounds consisting of a place name and the name of an event or period, are to be entered under the place name with the name of the event or period as subheading. The same order of components applies when the Place – Event (or Period) compound is part of a larger subject compound. A typical example would be

FIGHTERS, Aircraft, German, World War 2.

## NOTES AND REFERENCES

[1] The use of analysis of relationships between components as a means of determining component order owes its origin to Farradane, though in his system the relationships determine only a particular deductive order which is not necessarily that to be used in all alphabetical subject catalogues. Farradane's mistrust of the ambiguities of language is, however, too profound to permit him to countenance the approach attempted in this chapter.

[2] Kaiser, J. *Systematic indexing* (London, 1911).

[3] Ranganathan, S. R. *Library catalogue, fundamentals and procedure* (Madras, London, 1950).

# CHAPTER VII

# THE DICTIONARY CATALOGUE SINCE CUTTER

THIS chapter will attempt a brief survey of the trends in alphabetical subject cataloguing since Cutter, noting how in practice cataloguers have dealt with issues on which the guidance given in the *Rules for a dictionary catalog* is no longer adequate.

Such a survey must necessarily concern itself almost exclusively with the development of the American dictionary catalogue, because for most of this period United States practice provided the only authoritative dictionary catalogue technique for libraries of the English speaking world. If among British and Commonwealth dictionary cataloguers there were any who held independent views, they kept them to themselves. In the United States, the Library of Congress not only set up a great dictionary catalogue of its stock; from 1901 it began distributing printed catalogue cards bearing as tracings the subject headings used in this catalogue. Inevitably, something like a standardised practice has been achieved in libraries in the United States.

Library of Congress cards give tracings for subject entry headings. The demand for similar uniformity of practice in the matter of subject references led the Library of Congress to publish a complete list of its subject headings, including the references made to and from each heading. This list of subject headings later became the basis of Sears' *List of Subject Headings for small Libraries,*[1] which has been widely adopted both within and beyond the United States. Despite its bias toward American nomenclature and the fact that preferred British terms are not always included, Sears' *List* is still a basic working tool in many British libraries (and not only small ones) with dictionary catalogues. The Wilson *Cumulative Book Index* which circulates widely beyond the United States has its subject entries equipped with Library of Congress type of headings, and has also been instrumental in disseminating American dictionary catalogue practice in this country.

It would not be putting it too strongly to say that notwithstanding the phenomenal growth in dictionary catalogue organisation of the last half century, exploratory enquiry into the first principles of alphabetical subject cataloguing has languished. The Library of Congress has modelled its catalogue broadly on the basis provided by Cutter, but with a continuous series of modifications to meet new circumstances. Little or no attempt has been made to keep theory abreast of the developing practice, with the result that the present day *Subject Headings*[2] appears to embody a large number of purely arbitrary decisions, each of which can doubtless be justified when considered in isolation, but which do not form anything approaching an overall pattern of practice. It is never possible to predict from consideration of past decisions how the Library of Congress will deal with a new subject. In considering such methods we are necessarily confined to a rather sterile tract in the history of cataloguing, in which increasing standardisation of practice was achieved on the basis of a progressively attenuated body of principle. No hasty conclusions should be drawn from this on the demerits of standardisation as such. In any communications system conformity of practice with other systems has formidable advantages; but because of standardisation, habits may persist through sheer inertia and the size of the organisation they sustain, long after they should have been discarded.

Attempts at a comprehensive exposition of subject cataloguing as carried out during the Library of Congress era are not numerous. Margaret Mann in her *Introduction to cataloging and the classification of books*,[3] is content to be merely descriptive. Julia Pettee in *Subject headings: history and theory*[4] makes a more penetrating examination, but in the end commits herself only to the extent of offering a number of *ad hoc* solutions to isolated problems. On broad principles Miss Pettee did not venture beyond Cutter's position; in fact, despite the last word of her sub-title, she seems to have held almost as an article of faith the view that no further extended theoretical base for alphabetical subject cataloguing was possible. For questions not fully answered by Cutter, no further general rules could be laid down. Such issues were to be decided upon their merits (always assumed to be assessable) as they arose.

A briefer but rather more helpful account is given in *Subject headings: a practical guide* by D. J. Haykin.[5] This author at least appeared to recognise the need for comprehensive principles, though his attempts to rationalise some of the practices of the Library of Congress were often unconvincing.

### THE AMERICAN STANDARD SUBJECT HEADING LISTS

In addition to the books here mentioned, there are also the standard heading lists themselves, which throw a detailed light upon practice.[6]

The rest of this chapter will consist of a brief survey of some of the main features of the Library of Congress and Sears lists, helped out in places by the explanations of Haykin.

The standard subject heading lists are designed to produce an alphabetical subject catalogue broadly similar to that outlined in Chapter III, except that formal provision for references connecting used specific subjects to their containing generic subjects is omitted. As tools for practical cataloguing the lists have two purposes; first, to indicate which of a number of possible synonyms is to be used as a subject heading, and second, to show the references which are to be made to the chosen subject heading, from other subject headings in the list. Under each subject heading are given the terms *from which* references are made to it. They may be 'see' references from synonymous terms, or 'see also' references from related terms also used as subject headings. These 'see also' references are, in the main, from more general or co-ordinate topics. As a cross-check on the network of references each subject heading has also a list of related terms *to which* references are made from it. Such references from the chosen subject heading are not strictly necessary for practical work. They come into existence only when documents on the related subjects are being catalogued, and they will, of course, be signalled at the various list headings for the related subjects. The lists contain relatively few references from subordinate to more general topics. This is in accordance with the views of Cutter, who, it will be remembered, recoiled from the prospect of overloading the catalogue with specific-to-general references. It must, however, be repeated that the route from specific-to-general is the direction along which searches for information are commonly and appropriately conducted; and without specific-to-general references the alphabetical subject catalogue cannot bear comparison with the classified catalogue as a reference tool. There are logical objections to the use of the same directive 'see also' for generic-to-specific (downwards) references on the one hand and for specific-to-generic (upwards) and co-ordinate to co-ordinate references on the other. While the downward reference 'METALS *see also* URANIUM' means categorically that further material in the field of metals is to be found at the heading 'Uranium,' it is not necessarily true of the upwards reference 'URANIUM *see also* METALS' that further material on Uranium is to be found under the heading 'Metals'. To try to ensure that it is true, places an intolerable strain upon the tracings system, as each book on metals rather than the heading 'METALS' will have its own set of dependent references varying according to variations in scope of the subject covered. The upwards direction references would in fact take on the character of analytical subject entries rather than that of directions between headings. The difficulty can be resolved simply by the use of a more precise form of directive in each case. Downwards references could be given as 'For further material on Metals see Uranium', while the upwards and horizontal references would be 'For further material related to Uranium see Metals' and 'For material related to Plutonium see Uranium'.

The standard lists are obviously valuable to users of the Library of Congress cards. Each card bears the heading for the appropriate subject entry or entries, and the list supplies the data for constructing the necessary references, always provided that the heading on the card is not a new subject antedated by the latest edition of the list. The assistance which the standard lists provide to cataloguers not using Library of Congress cards is more dubious. Though they supply him with details of synonymous and related terms once he has formulated a subject heading, they offer no aid to the process of summarisation. Neither are they of much assistance in cataloguing a document of which the subject does not appear in the list. Absence of a term from the list may be attributable to any or several of the following reasons: (a) the term thought of by the cataloguer may be 'unestablished' in Cutter's sense. The subject cataloguer has therefore to classify the subject in order to arrive at a generic term. Unless he classifies within the framework of a definite classification scheme, there will often be innumerable possible generic terms which might be used; (b) the missing subject may be of more recent date than the last edition of the list; (c) in the case of Sears' *List* there remains the possibility that the subject has been excluded on the grounds that it is unlikely to be represented in a small library; (d) for the non-American cataloguer there is the possibility that the missing subject is entered only under an American term which he may not know.

When the cataloguer cannot find his term in the list, its absence cannot therefore be taken as a sign of unsuitability for use as a subject heading. The lists have little value as aids to the acquisition of consistent habits in subject cataloguing, they do not help in the formulation of correct subject headings, and they do not serve as checklists to be used to eliminate unsuitable headings. At best they reassure the cataloguer who thinks of one of the listed headings; though he is in need of such reassurance only because he has worked too long in a thicket of unexplained, *ad hoc*, and unpredictable decisions. They do, however, usefully assist the cataloguer who has thought of more than one satisfactory term for a subject heading and within their limits they may often remind him of synonyms that he has forgotten.

## LIBRARY OF CONGRESS PRACTICE

In an earlier chapter it was pointed out that the system of connective references, and the manner in which compound subjects are handled, together determine the essential character of an alphabetical subject catalogue. We may now take in turn each of these aspects of the Library of Congress list. We shall notice that the two aspects are not independent. Reference structure influences the manner in which compound subjects are treated and *vice versa*. Underlying ambiguities in both lurks that hesitancy in applying the principle of specific subject entry which springs from Cutter's attempt to distinguish 'established' subjects. D. J. Haykin recognised that the specific entry principle is applied in a limited fashion in Library of Congress practice, but added no further explanation beyond claiming that the non-specific entry policy is based on the experience of assisting readers. One suspects that the accumulation of a large amount of material on a generically entered subject often leads to a change to specific entry. Such a policy would be closely in line with Cutter's use of subdivisions to break up large numbers of entries under the same heading.

It has already been suggested that the effectiveness of a system of connective references depends upon the extent to which it is a system; that is to say upon the extent to which it is based upon a map of subjects symbolising their mutual relationships. A scheme of classification is just such a map, and we find that the Library of Congress list does appear to stem from such a classificatory background.

There seem to be two distinct and separate layers of relational references in the list. The first layer comprises a more or less complete network of downward directed hierarchical references and horizontally directed co-ordinate references, apparently based upon a classification scheme which often reveals the lineaments of the Decimal Classification. Superimposed upon this is a second layer of references, the content of which is unpredictable and apparently unrelated to any underlying principle. It would appear, according to Library of Congress reasoning, that a connective reference system based on classification alone does not suffice for a dictionary catalogue.

Miss Pettee, perhaps the most articulate expositor of the American type of dictionary catalogue, reveals a curiously ambivalent attitude to the whole question of the relationship between classification and subject cataloguing. On the one hand she affirms that the classificatory "horse" pulls the logical load of the alphabetical subject references in a dictionary catalogue, on the other she refers to the power of the dictionary catalogue to express relationships in several dimensions at once as its supreme advantage over the classified catalogue. Miss Pettee is right in stressing the multi-dimensional nature of subject relationships, but wrong, it may be thought, in supposing that the freedom of the alphabetical subject catalogue to set up multi-dimensional connective references is necessarily an advantage. Knowledge that such a miscellany of undefined relational dimensions exists is of no help to the subject cataloguer, whose whole task is to select a few of the possible lines of relationship to be embodied in 'see also' references. What the subject cataloguer requires above all are some principles defining and limiting those relationships which are to be expressed in references. Such questions are in current dictionary catalogue theory and practice put on one side in favour of casual selection in Miss Pettee's multi-dimensional continuum.

The multi-dimensional theory is evidently represented in Library of Congress practice by the superimposed or secondary layer of references mentioned above. A single example from the list will illustrate the two layers. At the heading 'Drawing', the following connective references are given:

Drawing

    See also  *Anatomy, Artistic
               Architectural drawing
               Blackboard drawing
               Brush drawing
               Caricature
               Charcoal drawing
               Crayon drawing
              *Design, Decorative
               Drawing books
               Drawings
               Figure drawing
               Geometrical drawing
              *Graphic methods
              *Human figure in art
              *Illustration of books
               Landscape drawing
               Map drawing
               Mechanical drawing
               Military sketching
               Painting

        Pastel drawing
        Pen drawing
        Pencil drawing
        *Perspective
        *Projection, Art
        *Proportion, Art
        *Shades and Shadows
        Topographical drawing

and Art

    Design, Decorative
    Illustration of books
    Manual training
    Perspective
        See also   Drawing

The items here asterisked are neither subordinate nor co-ordinate references. They are in fact the superimposed layer corresponding to the multi-dimensional linkages mentioned by Miss Pettee. It is worthwhile pausing to try and define the relationships of some of the asterisked headings to the concept 'Drawing'.

The idea to which they all have a common affiliation is that of Art. Drawing is a particular kind of Art which involves the placing of materials such as charcoal, crayon, etc. on a surface. Artistic Anatomy, Human Figure in Art, and Shades and Shadows are related to Art in a different manner. They are examples of what may be depicted in Art (not only in Drawing). Yet another kind of relationship with Art is suggested by the quartet Design, Decorative; Perspective; Projection, Art; Proportion, Art. Here we have neither a kind of Art nor what is depicted in Art, but some principles belonging to artistic activity and technique (again not limited to drawing alone). Finally we have Illustration of Books which is an example of a particular kind of Art being applied to an extraneous object. Here, then, we have four relational 'dimensions' radiating from Art and tentatively designated as Kind, Subject depicted, Principle of Activity, and Application. These are what Ranganathan would call separate 'facets' of the subject Art.

Now each of these topics is related to others in the other facets of Art indirectly through the common concept (Art) from which they spring. Any system of 'See also' references which tried directly to connect all these subjects would collapse under its own sheer volume. The Library of Congress list links together merely an indeterminate selection. Fortunately it is not necessary to represent indirect relationships by direct reference links.

Direct linkage between topics in different facets occurs when a compound subject (such as Perspective in Drawing, or the Human Figure in Book Illustration) is formed. But by its very nature a compound subject poses no problem of subject relationship which requires 'see also' references. It merely needs a set of references from each of those parts of the heading not used as entry word in the subject heading. Thus the heading 'Perspective, Drawing' and the supporting references from 'Drawing, Perspective' provide everything that is required to signal the relationship between Drawing and Perspective. 'See also' references are needed only to show relationships between those subjects which cannot (because they are in the same facet or in hierarchical relationship) form compound subjects. Why has this simplification of the pattern of 'see also' references evaded the compilers of the Library of Congress list? The reply to this question is to be found in the fact that except for a few special categories to be detailed later the list avoids compound subject headings as much as possible. This policy in turn stems back to Cutter's refusal of specific entry for non 'established' subjects. Semantically compound subjects are certainly, by and large, less 'established' than simple ones, and the general effect in Library of Congress practice is that a compound is often entered under one or more simple generic headings. Thus 'Perspective, Drawing' cannot apparently be admitted as an 'established' subject and books on this subject may expect to receive two generic entries under 'Perspective, Art' and 'Drawing' respectively. But double entry makes no contribution to signposting the relationship between Perspective and Drawing, hence it is necessary to make cross-references between the two headings. Undoubtedly many of the superimposed references compensate for the absence of compound subject headings.

A further consequence of the generic entry of 'unestablished' topics is that it is possible to have 'see' references from an unused specific term to a used generic one. Apparently there is a half-way condition of 'establishment' which warrants a reference but not an entry in the list. Thus we have 'Kneejerks see Reflexes', 'Public Libraries see Libraries', 'Dungeons see Prisons'. The opposite situation can also occur. 'See' references are made from certain generic terms which for unexplained reasons are not used as subject headings. Examples are 'Exports see Commerce' and 'Exports see Tariff'.

Not all terms listed as subject headings are included explicitly in the reference network. Names of concrete objects and materials are frequently not signalled by references from the generic headings which logically contain them. To a certain extent access to material on such subjects is made possible by the use of general references in the form:

Materials.    For special materials see under their names.

Such general references offer the possibility of vast economies both in respect of the actual size of the catalogue as well as in the tracings which need to be maintained. They fail, however, to provide for the collective enquiry which demands access to all the library's resources within a particular subject field. Probably their use in the Library of Congress list is confined to cases where intelligent anticipation suggests that collective enquiries are not likely to be made. As an aid to enquirers whose approach to a specific subject commences by resort to a generic term, the general reference is satisfactory provided that its use is limited to subjects of concrete character. To invite an enquirer to seek headings on 'the various aspects, kinds and applications' of say Biology would certainly fall short of reasonable subject catalogue service. Rather remotely allied to the general reference in Library of Congress is the scope note. This defines the range of meaning of a particular heading, and includes general directions for the finding of subjects which might conceivably be sought under the heading concerned but are in fact entered elsewhere.

Two further ways in which the reference-system of the Library of Congress list departs from the pattern outlined in Chapter III may be mentioned here. The reference pathway leading down from the generic to the specific does not always modulate. A direction may be given not only to the next subordinate term in the hierarchy, but also to a further subordinate term, one or more further stages down in the hierarchy. Thus we have both 'Economics see also Finance, Public', and 'Economics see also Taxation'. This practice is authorised by Cutter, but once again it is difficult to detect any rationale underlying its employment in some cases but not in others. It is not unknown for intermediate subordinate terms to be omitted altogether from the chain of references. Thus there is no reference linking Carving with Ice carving. The second peculiarity in Library of Congress practice is that 'see also' references between collateral subjects are sometimes unaccountably made in one direction only. Thus, we have 'Rime see also Rhythm', but not 'Rhythm see also Rime'.

Perhaps the chief lesson to be drawn from the referencing system in the Library of Congress list is that it is not enough for the purposes of the alphabetical subject catalogue to lay down the rule that collateral or co-ordinate subjects are to be linked by references. It is necessary to define with more precision just what collateral subjects are, otherwise the collateral relationship may be invoked to justify indiscriminate reference linkages. Examples of such false collateral references have been mentioned already in connection with the discussion on the heading 'Drawing' and its associated references. There are many others. Hygiene and Air are not a collateral pair, nor are Publicity and Journalism, nor Book Industries and Trades and Publishing and Publishers, nor Aesthetics and Classicism. The only possible closer definition of collateral relationship appears to lie within the concept of faceted classification. This will be discussed in the next chapter. Tentatively we may say that collateral relationship is restricted to terms which lie within the same facet of a given generic subject. The relationship between such a pair as Aesthetics and Classicism is almost always to be expressed by a compound subject heading (such as Classicism, Aesthetics). We shall now proceed to ascertain why this rarely happens in the Library of Congress list.

Compound subject headings are admitted in the list provided that they can be regarded as 'established'. Following Cutter, the Library of Congress usually enters phrases as they stand, inversion being an exceptional procedure. According to D. J. Haykin, every effort is made to avoid subheadings because they amount to 'indirect entry' which is supposedly incompatible with the specific entry principle. Some subjects are designated in ordinary language by a combination of words. We can, indeed we must, use such a combination as a subject heading in the alphabetical subject catalogue, and provided that the idea signified in the subject heading corresponds to that covered by the document in hand, we have specific subject entry. Such compound headings as 'Personnel Management' (phrase form) and 'Personnel, Management' (subheading form) are equally direct and specific for a document on personnel management. As it was pointed out in an earlier chapter, most subject headings with subheadings are really inverted phrases with the connecting preposition omitted. No doubt the dual reluctance of the Library of Congress to use either the inverted phrase form or the subheaded form springs from a common source. With regard to D. J. Haykin's appeal to directness it is difficult to see in what sense 'Air, Hygiene' is less direct than the two generic headings 'Air' and 'Hygiene' which would presumably replace the single compound heading in Library of Congress practice. The exact contrary would seem to be true. One objection to subheadings voiced both by Haykin and Margaret Mann suggests that their use is appropriate only to the alphabetico-classed catalogue. This is erroneous. The alphabetico-classed catalogue does provide indirect entry *via* a generic term, according to the scheme of subdivision and main classes adopted, irrespective of whether the subheading term standing alone could in fact represent the subject. This is an entirely different matter from the use of sub-headings in cases where there is no single word or phrase which denotes the subject. It is hardly an exaggeration to say that the reluctance to use subheadings is the greatest contributory factor to the deficiencies of the Library of Congress Catalogue as a reference tool.

In an effort to avoid the reproach of either non-specific entry or the use of subheadings, the Library of Congress sometimes uses phrase headings which from no point of view can be regarded as established. We find, for instance, 'Medicine, Magic, Mystic and Spagiric'. Another form of phrase without currency outside the list and its derivatives is the conjunctive form employed as a means of distinguishing homonyms. 'Files and Rasps' is an example of a phrase heading of this type. The second term 'Rasps' is a substitute for a qualifying subheading such as 'Tools' which is required to differentiate the files from the office equipment bearing the same name.

In the more recent editions of its list, the Library of Congress has found itself obliged to relax, to some extent, its veto on subject sub-headings. D. J. Haykin says that the purpose of these subheadings is "not to limit the subject but to provide for its arrangement". This is a mere play upon words; in the alphabetical subject catalogue the degree of subject specification and the mechanics of arrangement are simply two aspects of a single operation. One decides upon a particular heading and by the same token determines the position of the entry in the catalogue. Where such subject subheadings appear in the list, there is sometimes confusion because the same entry word is also part of one or more phrase headings. Thus we have

    Aeroplane racing

but

    Aeroplanes – Piloting

This weakness also appears in the Australian subject heading list of Sherrie and Jones, which has

    Animal ecology

but

    Animals – Behaviour

and

    Aeroplane engines

but

    Aeroplanes – Design

It is probably necessary to include both phrases and subject subheadings in dictionary catalogues, but there is a field of choice in deciding whether to use phrases whenever possible or subheadings whenever possible. The Library of Congress and those under its influence have chosen the former method for entangled reasons, which include intractable though indefinite reservations about the specific entry principle and what can only be emotional aversion from the superficial appearance of the alphabetico-classed catalogue. The alternative preference for subheadings with only a residuum of phrase headings was discussed and recommended in Chapter III.

The Library of Congress list also permits the use of form, chronological, and locality subheadings. The form subheadings, which include *subjects* such as societies and law, which classification schemes have for some time placed among common subdivisions, can be applied to any heading in the list. The time and place subheadings can only be used as headings where permission for their use is given. Haykin explains the procedure followed when literature occurs giving local treatment to a topic precluded in the list from taking a locality subheading. For example 'Gnatcatchers' is a term for which locality subheadings are not authorised. A book on 'Gnatcatchers of California' is given double entry as follows:

(1) Gnatcatchers
(2) Birds – California

The rule here appears to be that a second entry is made under the nearest generic term at which locality subheadings are allowed. It is hard to see what advantage is to be found in double non-specific entry over a single specific entry

Gnatcatchers – California

with inversion reference

California – Gnatcatchers. *See* Gnatcatchers – California

No doubt in evading specific subject entry in this fashion the Library of Congress Catalogue achieves a superficial appearance of simplicity. Under the generic heading or headings books covering the whole generic subject field are interspersed in random order with books on various sections of the field which possess no "established" subject name. Such lack of specification impedes the enquirer, whether he is seeking generic or specific subject material.

It may be useful to complete this chapter by mentioning a few further details of Library of Congress subject cataloguing practice which will serve to pin-point some minor practical problems not hitherto discussed.

The subheadings for historical periods in Library of Congress practice normally consist of verbal headings followed by dates: the latter are, however, the arranging symbols. The subheadings represent *ad hoc* historical eras worked out for particular subjects. Presumably historical specification in any field awaits the accumulation of a large amount of material under the heading. Historical episodes are normally entered under the place.

The form of geographical heading or subheading has exercised a great deal of the attention of Library of Congress cataloguers. In the first place there is the distinction to be made between ethnic adjectives and the names of places as such. The ethnic adjectives are used to name national schools in many of the fine arts, literature and philosophy. Usually they appear as the second word of an inverted phrase heading, e.g. 'Painting, English'. But in topics connected with language and literature the ethnic adjective is the first word, the phrase in this case not being inverted. The Sherrie and Jones list usefully treats some religious and period adjectives in exactly the same way as ethnic adjectives. Two further problems arise in connection with geographical headings proper. The first is concerned with the possible conflict between geographical names and the names of states. Library of Congress regularly prefers geographical names to political names on the ground of permanency. Against this must be placed the fact that political names are almost always better known, that they are usually more precise in meaning than geographical ones, and some denote areas which have no purely geographical name. The second problem is concerned with whether a locality subheading denoting an area within a country should be given directly or subordinated under country, giving such an entry as

Agriculture – France – Coutances

Directions for direct or indirect subordination are given in the list under each heading for which geographical subdivision is permitted. It is not possible to discern any controlling principle. The indirect method of subordination is contrary to specific entry and the result is a true alphabetico-classed entry. The motive for this practice is undoubtedly to link, say, 'Agriculture in France' with 'Agriculture in Coutances'. The alternative mechanism would of course be a 'see also' reference.

Agriculture – France, see also Agriculture – Coutances.

Any system of subheadings poses this problem, which is not peculiar to Library of Congress methods. Rigorous linkage of subheadings under the same heading by means of 'see also' references would be prohibitive for most catalogues and indexes. Perhaps here the general reference, reminding the enquirer in effect that the alphabetical subject catalogue does not physically group related topics, may come into its own. Thus the direction

> Agriculture – France. See also names of parts of France amongst these subheadings under Agriculture

would appear to meet all reasonable needs provided that the number of subheadings under the particular heading is not too great for scanning by the enquirer.

A situation which seems to challenge the whole principle of alphabetical arrangement arises when subheadings representing forms, periods, places and subjects appear together under a particular heading. Few dictionary catalogues are so firmly wedded to thoroughgoing alphabetical arrangement that they would arrange all subheadings in a single sub-sequence. Conventional practice attempts grouping of kinds of subheadings and arrives at some such arrangement as the following:

HEADING
References from Heading
Subheadings
    – Forms
    – Periods
    – Places
    – Subjects

Library of Congress, in its current annual subject catalogues, adopts a simpler scheme, namely:

HEADING
References from Heading
Subheadings
    – Forms, Periods (introduced by the term 'History') and Subjects
      in one sequence
    – Places
Heading as first word of an inversion

With this final passing glance at a particular sector of the alphabetical catalogue structure, at which the alphabetical principle appears to be insufficient, we conclude the survey of this form of catalogue considered mainly from the point of view of heading language. Reference has been made from time to time to the relevance of classification for all forms of subject catalogues; its importance as the foundation of attempts to signal subject relationship has been underlined, though not treated in any detail. In the remainder of this book it will become clear that classification has also a contribution to make to the problem of the rendering of compound subjects for which no preferred customary nomenclature exists. In the chapter immediately following, an approach is made by way of a consideration of two forms of the systematic or classified catalogue, and – most important for our purpose – their supporting alphabetical subject indexes. We shall later proceed to enquire whether existing general classification schemes can be applied directly to the construction of alphabetical subject catalogues.

## NOTES AND REFERENCES

[1] Sears, M. E. *List of subject headings*, edited by B. M. Frick (New York, 1954).

[2] Library of Congress. *Subject headings used in the dictionary catalogs of Library of Congress*, edited by Marguerite V. Quattlebaum (Washington, 1957).

[3] Mann, M. *Introduction to cataloging and the classification of books* (Chicago, 1943).

[4] Pettee, J. *Subject headings* (New York, 1946).

[5] Haykin, D. J. *Subject headings* (Washington, 1951).

[6] No mention has been made of the very large number of subject heading lists for special subjects which appeared in the period under review. Among these the lists issued by the Special Libraries Association are prominent. The library of the Library Association holdings include lists on religion, education, industrial relations, architecture, music, literature, chemistry, nuclear physics, engineering and medicine.

[7] Sherrie, H. & Jones, P. M. *Short list of subject headings* (Sydney, 1950).

## CHAPTER VIII

## THE CONTRIBUTION OF CLASSIFICATION

THE classified, or systematic, catalogue uses the physical collocation of entries for related subjects as a means of signalling subject relationship. Instead of connecting allied topics by references, it assembles them together, in so far as this is possible in a linear sequence. Such a placing together of related subjects necessitates a scheme of arrangement. No scheme of subject arrangement can be comprehended instantly in all its details by an enquirer, except the purely alphabetical. Accordingly, an alphabetical subject index is required to give the enquirer access to that portion of the classified sequence of entries which is relevant to his enquiry. It follows, therefore, that while the classified catalogue appears to escape some of the problems associated with connective references, it requires a subject index which is just as critically concerned with the construction of composite subject headings as is the alphabetical subject catalogue discussed in earlier chapters.

### THE SUBJECT INDEX – ADAPTING DICTIONARY CATALOGUE HEADINGS

It is possible to construct headings for the subject index according to the practice for alphabetico-specific catalogues already outlined. Indeed it might be argued that the headings should be the same both for the alphabetical subject catalogue and for the classified catalogue subject index, seeing that both are intended to match the initial approach-ideas of the enquirer. These ideas will remain the same whichever form of catalogue confronts the enquirer.

Any attempt to adapt for subject index purposes lists intended for alphabetical subject catalogues encounters two major difficulties. These are not insurmountable, but they are sufficiently daunting to discourage experimentation. The first is that all of the classification schemes so far available are less elaborated than the ideas they are designed to accommodate, so that in practice there are always subjects for which no specific classification symbol is provided. For want of any better procedure they are placed under the narrowest subject which will contain them, and for which the classification scheme has a symbol. The enquirer consulting the subject index for one of these unspecified subjects is given a particular location in the classified file but the material he finds under the symbol quoted is mostly of a more general nature than the subjects he requires. The material on the wanted subject is indeed somewhere within the area of the symbol given, but it is dispersed among documents of a more general subject nature because under any given classification symbol the normal sub-arrangement is by author or date. The basic remedy is easy to state, but not so easy to carry out without some practical knowledge of classification making by facet analysis. It is to sub-arrange by subject, so that even if the topic required has no specific symbol, the material on it is at least presented together as a distinct section of the classified sequence. Effective sub-arrangement of unspecified subjects under a generic symbol is tantamount to expansion of the classification scheme. It does not, however, necessarily call for the provision of a corresponding supplementary notation. Material on an unspecified subject can be displayed as a group merely by being given a verbal subject heading. The major disadvantage of reliance upon such verbal specification is, of course, that it has no ordinal value; when a number of purely verbal feature headings are used under a given classification symbol, there is no way of mechanising their arrangement into the best order. Furthermore though the non-specified subjects may be entered in the subject index, the direction can be given only to the containing generic subject which has been assigned notation. It is one of the curiosities of cataloguing history that until quite recently the compilers of classified catalogues felt no need to provide on individual entries a verbal interpretation of the class symbol. In consequence the arrangement was often even less comprehensible to readers than the tangled classification order necessarily dictated.

The second difficulty in adapting dictionary catalogue subject heading lists for classified catalogue subject indexes is to determine what role, if any, dictionary catalogue connective references should play in the subject index. They are clearly redundant in the form in which they are used in the dictionary catalogue. Nevertheless the relationships they signify should also be demonstrated in some fashion in the classified catalogue. In the last chapter it was shown that the standard lists do not attempt to distinguish between the various kinds of 'see also' references. Anyone attempting adaptation for the classified catalogue subject index would first of all need to differentiate between (*a*) generic-to-specific and (*b*) collateral references and (*c*) false collateral references, as described in the last chapter in connection with the heading 'Drawing'. Generic-to-specific references can be admitted to the subject index *as entries* in two possible forms. They can be converted into entries with subheadings. Thus the reference 'Printing see also Typography' becomes

    [1]Printing: Typography    655.25    (D.C. Notation)

This method can be used irrespective of whether the generic-to-specific hierarchy represented in the reference corresponds to a similar hierarchy in the classification scheme. Thus the reference 'Books see also Bibliography' is rendered in the subject index as

    Books: Bibliography    010.

The fact that the Decimal classification does not place Bibliography within the generic class Books does not preclude the appearance of the entry in the subject index. The alternative method is to make, not a subheaded entry directing to the specific subject, but a simple generic entry under the wider term from which (in an alphabetical catalogue) a 'see also' reference would be made. The entries thus produced would read

| | | |
|---|---|---|
| Typography | 655.25 | (Specific) |
| Printing | 655 | (Generic) |
| Technology | 600 | (Generic) |

This method of converting 'see also' references for subject index use moves away from the conception of the subject index as a list of specific subject entries. The entry 'Printing 655' does not state categorically that there is a book on printing in the catalogue. It merely indicates that there is material dealing with a subject within the field of printing, which may or may not include a book on printing in general. As a technique it works satisfactorily as long as the chain of generic-to-specific references given in the standard list corresponds to the hierarchy of terms in the classification scheme. A subject can, as Miss Pettee[2] has emphasised, belong to more than one hierarchy in the dictionary catalogue, but to one alone in the classified catalogue. In such cases a corresponding linkage can be made in the classified catalogue by means of a 'see also' cross reference in the classified file itself. Thus for a Dewey classified catalogue the reference 'Bibliography see also Printing' would have no equivalent entry in the subject index, but would appear in the classified file as follows:

    010 – Bibliography.  See also 655 – Printing

A reference in the opposite direction from 655 to 010 would also be desirable.

    'See also' references in the alphabetical subject catalogue between collateral subjects frequently correspond to subjects collocated in the classified sequence. Where this is not the case the subjects concerned are linked together in the classified section by means of a two-way 'see also' cross reference. Nothing corresponding to 'see also' references between collateral subjects is required for the subject index.

It will be seen that irrespective of alternative methods of procedure the use of dictionary catalogue standard lists for constructing the subject index to a classified catalogue is fraught with complications. The references given in the lists must first be sorted out according to the kind of linkage they represent, generic-to-specific, collateral-to-collateral, and collateral-to-false collateral. The terms from which generic-to-specific linkages are made are then brought into the subject index in one form or another. If the subheaded form is used, all such generic-to-specific subject references can be represented in the subject index as entries. If the alternative method involving the indexing of generic terms without subheadings is used, then only those 'see also' references corresponding to the hierarchy of terms in the classification will appear as entries in the subject index. 'See also' references not corresponding to subjects collocated in the classification scheme will appear as two-way 'see also' references in the classified sequence of entries. The following table shows the correspondences between the various kinds of 'see also' references in the alphabetical subject catalogue and equivalent mechanisms in the classified catalogue and its alphabetical index.

| Alphabetical subject catalogue | Classified catalogue index with subheadings | Classified catalogue index without subheadings |
|---|---|---|
| 'See also' references generic-to-specific, corresponding to hierarchy in classification scheme | Specific entries in subject index | Generic and specific entries in index |
| 'See also' references generic-to-specific, not corresponding to hierarchy in classification scheme | Specific entries in subject index | No entry in subject index. 'See also' cross-reference in classified file |
| 'See also' references collateral-to-collateral. Corresponding to subjects collocated in the classification scheme | No subject index entry | No subject index entry |
| 'See also' references collateral-to-collateral. Subjects not collocated in the classification scheme | No subject index entry. 'See also' cross-reference in classified file | No entry in subject index. 'See also' cross-reference in classified file |

## PUBLISHED INDEXES OF CLASSIFICATION SCHEMES

In view of the amount of manipulation of 'see also' references required, as well as the need to elaborate the classification scheme, it is hardly surprising that few libraries with classified catalogues have seriously faced the problem of converting dictionary catalogue data into subject index entries. Many classified catalogues have no subject index to the material in the classified file. In many cases it is felt sufficient to rely upon the published index to the classification scheme in use. Quite apart from the particular merits or otherwise of these indexes there are two fairly obvious drawbacks to their use as indexes to classified catalogues. In the first place many subjects are likely to be indexed in the scheme which are not represented in the library stock or catalogue, and enquirers, after experience of a system which appears, as it were, to fade out half-way, are not likely to feel any great confidence in the index. The second objection springs from the opposite situation in which the library possesses material for which the classification makes no specific place. Few of these topics are cited in the indexes to the schemes which make no provision for them, and hence no information is given to enquirers as to their existence in the library stock. This is not, however, to deny the contribution which some of the indexes to classification schemes have made to the rationale of subject indexing. In particular, mention must be made of the index to the Dewey Decimal Classification which anticipates some of the features of the only systematic subject indexing technique so far devised – the 'chain procedural' method of Ranganathan. Whether Dewey consciously appreciated that his index collocated related topics not assembled together in the Classification Table remains doubtful; but it is difficult to assign any alternative sense to the word 'relativ'.[3] The fact that the relative index has frequently been invoked almost as a justification for poor collocation of subjects in the Decimal Scheme should not obscure the general validity of the conception of the subject index as an exhibitor of subject relationships not embodied in the classified sequence. It has already been noted (table opposite p. 30) that some accidental collocation of related subjects occurs in alphabetical subject cataloguing; and in connection with the Kaiser scheme it was shown that logical analysis of terms of complex meaning widens the degree of such collocation. The related terms Wages and Labour Disputes can be collocated in an alphabetical sequence by logical analysis as

Labour – Costs
Labour – Disputes

### CLASSIFICATION AS A DETERMINANT OF COMPONENT ORDER

In indexing the Decimal Classification it was discovered, as has already been noticed here in the discussion on compound subjects in the alphabetical subject catalogue, that complex subjects without established names can be rendered only by some form of recitation of the elementary terms which make up the complex concept. In Chapter VI a great deal of attention was given to the order in which the constituent terms should be cited in a compound subject heading. Significance of meaning and the kind of relationship between the terms were suggested as determinants of order. In the index to the Decimal Classification an entirely new principle for ordering the elementary terms of a subject compound was adduced from the hierarchical structure of the classification scheme itself. Briefly, the terms of compound subjects (other than established phrases) are arranged in hierarchical order, specific to general, and usually entered in that form alone. On this principle we might expect 'Surgery of the arm' to be entered as

    Arm surgery      617.57

The hierarchical structure of the classification scheme in the area concerned is as follows:

    Medicine          610
      Surgery          617
        Regional         617.5
          Upper extremities  617.57
            Arm            617.57 (requires specific notation)

Each of these terms is an entry word, which may require to be qualified by one or more of the terms preceding it on the hierarchical ladder.

    The corresponding set of subject index entries would read:

    Medicine 610
    Surgery 617
    Regional surgery 617.5
    Upper extremities surgery 617.57
    Arm surgery      617.57

(In the actual index to the 14th edition of D.C. 'Arm surgery' does not appear because there is no specific notation for it. 'Regional surgery' is also omitted, but appears as 'Surgery Regional'). In the example above, the combined terms happen to be ordered according to the criteria laid down in Chapter VI, except in the case of Regional surgery, which would have been inverted. Sometimes a fully established phrase may become inverted when rendered in ascending hierarchical order. For instance 'Business correspondence' becomes

    Correspondence    Commercial meth.    office econ.    651.7

In such cases the D.C. index often provides a further entry in the uninverted form. In fact the whole application of the technique is flexible and apparent deviations may be readily found.

It may perhaps be doubted whether the constituent terms of any compound subject can always be viewed as terms in a hierarchical ladder. That this doubt should appear is due partly to the incompleteness of the schedules, both in degree of specification and of proper modulation of the hierarchical stages. In the above example 'Limbs' has been omitted from the chain of generic classes, and would be missed in any purely automatic application of the method. These are, however, faults and deficiencies of a particular classification scheme. In a fully faceted classification the correspondence between classificatory hierarchy and compound subject terms is, as will be seen in the next chapter, much more apparent.

The general effect of the Dewey method of subject indexing is that the index does not usually give under a given subject those subdivisions which appear under it in the classification scheme. The preface to the 14th edition of the Decimal Classification (p. 13) describes its method in this way.

"All topics in blakface typ in Index are further divided in the Tables, where one may see the subheds. This saves reprinting all these subdivisions which wud increase Index bulk many-fold; e.g. if one having a book on 'prison labor' looks in the index for 'Convict Labor' . . . he finds at once its special number 331.51; but if on the other hand he thinks to look only for jeneral subject 'Labor', he finds in blakface type the entry 'Labor, political econ. 331', and turning to Tables he finds under 331 the subdivision '331.51 Convict labour'." The practical result of all this may be envisaged by comparing portions of the indexes of the Dewey and Bliss[4] classifications, under the term "Chemistry".

Bliss's index has about ninety subheadings under Chemistry, of which the following are typical:

| | |
|---|---|
| Chemistry | C – CA |
|    Analytical | CG |
|       Industrial | CTT |
|       Microscopic | CGG |
|       Organic | COG |
|       Qualitative | CGL |
|       Quantitative | CGQ |
|       Technical | CTT |
|    Apparatus for chemical study | CAQ |
|    Applications of | C54 |

| | |
|---|---|
| Applied chemistry | CT – CTA |
| Calculations in | |
|     Analytical chemistry | CG8 |
|     Electrochemistry | CEC |
|     Physical chemistry | CB8 |
| Compounds | CID; CO |
| History of | C3 |
| Industries | CTM; CU |
| Inorganic substances, compounds | CI; CN |
| Manufactures | CTM; CU |
| Organic | CO |
| Physical | CB |

The index under the same heading from the 14th edition of the Decimal Classification contains thirty-three subheadings, such as the following:

| | | |
|---|---|---|
| Chemistry | | 540 |
| | Agricultural agronomy | 630.24 |
| | **analytic** | **543** |
| | and photographic theory | 770.54 |
| | **physics** | **541.3** |
| | religion nat. theol. | 215 |
| | **animal** | **547** |
| | zoology | 591.19 |
| | **applied** | **660** |
| | **botany** | **581.19** |
| | **cosmic astronomy** | **523** |
| | dairy industry | 637.127 |
| | early alchemy | 540.1 |

The most obvious difference between the two excerpts is that the items in Bliss's index all refer to the same general area of the classification, namely that represented by the symbol C, whereas Dewey's entries mostly direct to locations *outside* 540 – Chemistry. All of Bliss's ninety odd entries refer to positions within the class C – Chemistry, whereas only ten of Dewey's thirty-three entries refer to the class 540 – Chemistry. The disparity is only partly attributable to Bliss's greater success in collecting more aspects of chemistry into a single area of his scheme. It follows from the deliberate policy of the Dewey index in restricting entry of subheadings under a subject, which are also subdivisions of the subject in the classification scheme. The other point to be noted is the difference in the actual number of entries required under each system. Again the difference between Bliss's ninety entries and Dewey's thirty-three is only partly accounted for by the greater degree of specification in Bliss's scheme. Many of the subheadings he lists are represented in the Dewey classification but not indexed under the policy already described. The resultant economy is considerable. In this connection it should be borne in mind that, since the order of constituent terms of compound subjects is determined by their respective places in the classification hierarchy, permutations need not occur, except on occasions where the technique results in the inversion of an established phrase. An idea of the scale of saving through the avoidance of subject index permutations may be given by a further example. A three-element subject, such as Sanitary engineering in mines, would receive entries on the lines of the following:

Engineering   620

Sanitation engineering   628

Industrial sanitation engineering   628.5

Mines sanitation engineering   628.51922

giving a total of four entries, three of which would also do duty whenever any further subject in the respective fields of Industrial sanitation engineering, Sanitary engineering, or Engineering appeared for indexing. If we attempt to provide specific entry approaches by permutation of the constituent terms, we require

| Mines, Sanitation, Engineering | 628.51922 |
| Sanitation, Engineering, Mines | 628.51922 |
| Engineering, Mines, Sanitation | 628.51922 |
| Mines, Engineering, Sanitation | 628.51922 |
| Sanitation, Mines, Engineering | 628.51922 |
| Engineering, Sanitation, Mines | 628.51922 |

If we were providing a similar approach from Industrial sanitation engineering, without subheading we should require six further permuted subject index entries; if we wished to employ the generic term with subheadings method (Industrial sanitation engineering, Mines) we should need twenty-four further entries. And in neither case would any of the entries be of further use in connection with other subjects in Industrial sanitation engineering, Sanitary engineering, or Engineering.

One further point remains to be mentioned. The order of citing terms forming a compound will vary according to the structure of the classification scheme. The hierarchical steps of the earlier example, Surgery of the Arm, might be arranged differently in another classification, as for instance

Medicine
    Regions of the body
        Upper limbs
            Arm
                Surgery

producing index entries as follows:

Surgery, Arm
Arm, Medicine
Upper limb, Medicine
Regions of the body
Medicine

The combinations are all different from those resulting from the Dewey structure, but the entry or approach words are identical, apart from the transformation of "Regional" into "Regions".

## RANGANATHAN'S CHAIN PROCEDURE

Ranganathan's chain procedure[5] may be described as a more coherent and rigorous application of the methods hit upon by Dewey in his search for economy. The components of all compound subjects are cited in specific-to-general order: therefore it follows that no term can have as index subheadings the subdivisions which appear under it in the classification schedule. There is no need for such distinctions as "Blakface typ", as any concept indexed may prove to be subdivided in the classification schedule. There is no multiple entry of the same compound by permutation of components, though Ranganathan has sometimes sanctioned additional entries under established phrases in what amounts to generic-specific order. As far as possible all adjectives are replaced by their corresponding substantives, and the completed subject index relates by collocation various aspects of subjects not brought together in the classification scheme.

## THE EXTENDED ROLE OF THE SUBJECT INDEX

In any alphabetical subject index to a classification, some related subjects separated in the classification will be brought together through verbal similarities. This occurs in a somewhat haphazard and arbitrary fashion because single words often stand for complex ideas. If all ideas could be represented in the index only by means of combinations of elementary constituent terms, collocation in index sequence would signal relationships comprehensively. Chain procedure indexing, reflecting the modulated structure of the classification scheme, tends to represent complex ideas by means of elementary combined terms rather than by single complex terms: because of this, the coverage of subject relationship signalled by a classified catalogue supported by collocation of terms in the chain procedure index is probably greater than that produced by any alternative method of indexing. It is superior, in this respect, to the purely alphabetical catalogue relying on the hazards of natural language collocation. Because it shows relationship between a genus and its included species, it would also be superior to an alphabetical catalogue which succeeded in reducing all complex ideas to combinations of elementary terms.

The subject index began as a necessary ancillary to the classified file of entries. It was alone a key to the location of subjects within the classified file. As such it had to face the question of the order in which the verbal components of complex subjects should be given in the index entries. The solution of this problem based on the structure of the classification scheme involved the resolution of the verbal components into separate semantic units, each corresponding to the "difference" added at each step down the hierarchy. The method also called for the indexing of generic concepts (as an alternative to the permutation of the terms comprising the specific subject). This in turn produced an index structure which collocated related subjects not brought together in the classification scheme or classified file. The subject index has thus assumed an extended role as a complementary mechanism for showing subject relationship.

## MULTIPLE CLASSIFIED ENTRY AND SIMPLE TERM INDEX

We must now notice an alternative development of the classified catalogue in which the role of the subject index remained static, precisely because the complementary mechanism for showing subject relationship was to be found in the classified file of entries itself. This form of classified catalogue is fairly typical of those found in special libraries classified by the Universal Decimal Classification.[6] Many of these catalogues are in fact made without an index, except perhaps the index to the U.D.C. scheme. Multiple entry in the classified file is the answer given in this form of classified catalogue to the problem of subject relationships which are not explicit in the classification scheme. Thus a document upon a compound subject is entered under the class number of each component relevant to the special subject field of the library concerned. The synthetic notation of the U.D.C. scheme helps to make this policy of multiple entry an automatic process. Thus if the subject is the Thermodynamics of Fluid Flow the class number is constructed by combining the symbols for Fluid Flow (532.5) and

Thermodynamics (537.6) as 532.5: 536.7. The cataloguer then makes a routine permuted entry at 536.7: 532.5. The practice of multiple entry as a means of overcoming the limitations of a linear classification scheme in the representation of relationship, is closely allied to the practice already noted of making "see also" references between physically separated, but logically related, sections of the classified file.

This method of showing subject relationship by means of multiple entry in the classified file works fairly well in catalogues limited in subject scope because, within a narrow field, the number of aspects of a given subject from which enquirer approaches are to be expected is reasonably limited. It is not, of course, merely a question of making an entry under each component of the compound subject, but of supplying entries for such permutations of the terms as are considered relevant to anticipated enquirer approach. Thus the topic 'Thermodynamics of Fluid Flow as applicable to hydraulic machines' is represented in U.D.C. notation, by the following composite class symbol, each element of which stands for one of the three components of the subject:

532.5 : 536.7 : 621.22

Full rendering of the relationships here would involve six entries under the following symbols:

532.5   : 536.7   : 621.22
532.5   : 621.22  : 536.7
536.7   : 532.5   : 621.22
536.7   : 621.22  : 532.5
621.22  : 532.5   : 536.7
621.22  : 536.7   : 532.5

Such a method would be quite impracticable for a general subject catalogue. Where it is employed in a special library catalogue, it requires an alphabetical index which need consist of simple terms only, since all significant combinations which include a particular component will be found in a single place in the classified file.

As most classified catalogue structures of this kind are associated with the U.D.C., it is not altogether easy to evaluate them apart from the particular merits and demerits of that scheme. The arrangement achieved by the use of the U.D.C. colon, which stands for any kind of relationship, is often arbitrary, without coherent pattern, and unhelpful. It is, however, possible to conceive of a more rationally constructed synthetic classification scheme being used for a catalogue of this type. It would be possible, for instance, to devise a scheme based on Ranganathan's or Vickery's[7] facet formula and permitting full permutation of the facets. Thus a compound subject would be entered in the classified file, not only in the order P, M, E, S, T, but also in the other 119 possible permutations of the five facets. The results would be greatly superior to most sections of the U.D.C. We should have, in effect, a series of 120 faceted schemes arranged one after the other and all offering a different pattern of division of the subject field concerned. This would, of course, be a serviceable but expensive tool for dealing with the collective type of enquiry.

### ALPHABETICAL AND CLASSIFIED FORMS –PLACING THE HIATUS

In the early part of this book repeated emphasis was given to the underlying identity of structure and purpose of the alphabetical and classified forms of subject catalogue. We are now in a position to lay our finger upon the essential point of their divergence in method, particularly as this affects enquiry procedure.

By adequate analysis and permutation of compound subjects, and by using a system of connective references based upon a classification scheme, an alphabetical subject catalogue may make it possible for an enquirer to gather together *everything* (within the limits of the indexing units employed) in the catalogue about a given subject, simple or compound, and about allied subjects which lie, as it were, just beyond its boundaries. The connective reference employed by the alphabetical subject catalogue is in effect a prompter. It says "Search under a particular heading *and then* you will find material on a subject related to this one."

In the case of the classified catalogue, access to any subject requires a prompter in the shape of the subject index, which says to the reader "Go to this class symbol *and then* you will find both this subject and its relations physically together". Neither of the two forms of catalogue avoids the hiatus represented above by "*and then*". The alphabetical catalogue inserts the hiatus between entries on a subject and those on related subjects. The classified catalogue inserts the hiatus before *all* enquiries whether for specific material or of collective character; by this means it avoids placing a hiatus between entries on a particular subject and those on a related subject. Only the ideal catalogue, with permuted class symbols and multiple entry for compound subjects avoids the hiatus between a subject and *all* its relations. The classified catalogue structure described earlier with chain procedure index eliminates the hiatus between a subject and a limited number of its important relatives alone. The less important relatives can be found, but by way of a double hiatus, which might be expressed as the basic direction to enquirers "For further related subjects, go back to the index to the term which directed you here *and then* you may find other aspects or subject contexts of this term listed there. Go to the various class numbers as directed by these entries *and then* you will find the further related material".

THE TWO FORMS OF CLASSIFIED CATALOGUE COMPARED

The two forms of classified catalogue and subject index structure described above are demonstrated in the two examples of subject layout which follow. It is assumed that a small collection of material on Library Science is catalogued first for a non-permuted single entry classified catalogue with chain procedure subject index, and second for a multiple entry permuted classified catalogue with elementary terms subject index. Neither subject index includes synonyms in this model. The underlying facet structure of the classification scheme is the same in both cases.

## Non-permuted single entry structure with chain procedure subject index.

Classified file – subject sequence

### LIBRARIES

**Organisation and administration**
  Records
  Finance
    Accounts
  Buildings
  Staff
    Finance

**Library stock – processes**
  Finance
  Selection
  Records
  Binding
    Buildings
  Classification
  Assistance to readers

**Library stock – varieties**
  By form
    Periodicals
  By subject
    Biology
      Periodicals

**Libraries and users**
  Rules for users
  Services by kind of access to material
    Lending services
    Reference services
    Copying services

**Kinds of libraries by owners**
  Central government
    Staff
  Local authorities
    Buildings
    Staff
      Finance
    Stock
  County libraries
  Municipal libraries
    Lending services
    Reference services
      Staff
  Firms

**Kinds of libraries by owners – cont.**
  Firms – cont.
    Stock
      Periodicals
    Private libraries
      Stock
      Selection
      Classification
**Kinds of libraries by group served**
  Sociological group
    Prisoners
      Stock
        Periodicals

**Kinds of libraries by group served – cont.**
  Prisoners – cont.
    Local authority service
      Stock
        Selection
  Subject interest group
    Medical profession
      Stock
        Encyclopaedias
      Lending service
      Reference service
        Stock
          Classification

In this subject sequence compound subjects are cited only once in the reverse order of the subject sequence, so that in effect any subject can be divided like the preceding sequence as far as applicable. Thus, for instance, the above subdivision of Libraries for Prisoners and Medical libraries follows the order of topics in the earlier part of the subject sequence. Or to put the matter in another way, any topic treated from a general standpoint in the early part of the sequence may appear lower as a component of a compound. The subjects, simple and compound, listed above in systematic order require the following subject index built up on chain procedure:

Accounts
Administration
Assistance to readers
Binding
Biology : Stock
Buildings
Buildings : Binding
Buildings : Local authority libraries
Central government libraries
Classification
Classification : Private libraries
Classification : Reference works : Medical libraries
Copying services
County libraries
Encyclopaedias : Stock : Medical libraries
Finance
Finance : Staff
Finance : Staff : local authority libraries
Finance : Stock
Firm libraries
Lending services
Lending services : Medical libraries
Lending services : Municipal libraries
Local authority libraries
Local authority libraries : Prison services
Medical libraries
Municipal libraries
Organisation
Periodicals : Biology : Library stock
Periodicals : Stock
Periodicals : Stock : Firm libraries
Periodicals : Stock : Prison libraries
Prison libraries
Private libraries
Records
Records : Stock
Reference services

Reference services : Medical libraries
Reference services : Municipal
 libraries
Rules for users
Selection : Stock
Selection : Stock : Local authority
 libraries : Prison services
Selection : Stock : Private libraries
Staff
Staff : Central government libraries
Staff : Reference services : Municipal
 libraries

Stock
Stock : Firm libraries
Stock : Local authority libraries
Stock : Local authority libraries :
 Prison services
Stock : Medical libraries
Stock : Prison libraries
Stock : Private libraries
Stock : Reference services : Medical
 libraries

This sample of material requires 51 subject terms in the classified file,
and 54 entries in the subject index.

## Permuted multiple entry structure with subject index of simple terms.

### Classified file – subject sequence

#### LIBRARIES

**Organisation and administration**
  Records
    Stock
  Finance
    Accounts
    Staff
      Local authority libraries
    Stock
    Local authority libraries
      Staff
  Buildings
    Binderies
    Local authorities
  Staff
    Finance
      Local authority libraries
    Reference service
    Local authority libraries
      Municipal libraries
    Central government libraries
    Local authority libraries
      Finance
      Municipal libraries
        Reference services

**Library stock – processes**
  Finance
  Selection
    Local authority services
      Prison libraries
    Private libraries
    Prison libraries
      Local authority services
  Records
  Binding
    Buildings
  Classification
    Reference stock
      Medical libraries
    Private libraries
    Medical libraries
      Reference stock
  Assistance to readers

**Library stock – varieties**
  By form
    Periodicals
      Biology
      Firm libraries
      Prison libraries

**Library Stock – varieties – cont.**
  Encyclopaedias
    Medical libraries
  By subject
    Biology
      Periodicals

**Library stock for special purposes and kinds of libraries**
  Reference Stock
    Classification
      Medical libraries
    Medical libraries
      Classification
  Local authority services
    Selection
      Prison libraries
    Prison libraries
      Selection
  Firm libraries
    Periodicals
  Prison libraries
    Selection
    Periodicals
      Local authority services
    Local authority services
      Selection
  Private libraries
    Selection
    Classification
  Medical libraries
    Classification
      Reference stock
    Encyclopaedias
    Reference stock
      Classification

**Libraries and users**
  Rules for users
  Services by kind of access to materials
    Lending service
      Local authority libraries
        Municipal libraries
      Medical libraries
    Reference services

**Libraries and users – cont.**
  Reference services – cont.
    Staff
      Local authorities
        Municipal libraries
    Stock
      Classification
        Medical libraries
    Local authorities
      Staff
    Medical libraries
      Stock
        Classification
    Copying services

**Kinds of library service by owner**
  Central government
    Staff
  Local authority
    Finance
    Staff
    Buildings
    Staff
      Finance
    County
    Municipal
      Staff
        Reference service
        Lending service
        Reference service
          Staff
      Prison service
        Stock
          Selection
          Periodicals
    Firm library
      Stock
        Periodicals
    Private library
      Stock
        Selection
        Classification

**Kind of library service by group served**
  Sociological groups
    Prison libraries

| Kind of library service by group served – cont. | Kind of library service by group served – cont. |
|---|---|
| Prison libraries – cont. | Subject interest groups |
|   Stock |   Medical libraries |
|     Selection |     Stock |
|       Local authority service |       Classification |
|     Periodicals |         Reference works |
|     Local authority service |       Encyclopaedias |
|     Selection |       Reference works |
|   Local authority service |         Classification |
|     Stock |   Lending services |
|       Selection |   Reference services |
| |     Stock |
| |       Classification |

This permuted classified sequence requires the following alphabetical subject index:

| | |
|---|---|
| Accounts | Lending services |
| Administration | Local authority libraries |
| Assistance to readers | Medical libraries |
| Binding | Municipal libraries |
| Biology : Stock | Organisation |
| Buildings | Periodicals : Stock |
| Central government services | Prison libraries |
| Classification | Private libraries |
| Copying services | Reference services |
| County libraries | Rules for users |
| Encyclopaedias : Stock | Selection : Stock |
| Finance | Staff |
| Firm libraries | Stock |

In this sample, assuming there were one document per subject quoted, the permuted classified sequence would contain 2.68 times as many entries as the non-permuted scheme. On the other hand the simple term subject index to the permuted scheme has only half the number of entries as the chain procedure index to the non-permuted scheme. Because index entries containing no identifying details of particular documents are necessarily briefer than entries in the classified catalogue, the saving produced by the non-permuted structure is substantial in this case, though not spectacular. It is obvious, however, that the disparity in size of the two kinds of catalogue will increase steeply according to the number of documents on compound subjects added, as well as on the actual proportion and complexity of compound subjects to simple subjects represented.

## NOTES AND REFERENCES

[1] The class numbers cited and Relative Index entries given as from the Decimal Classification are taken from the 14th edition of that scheme, with occasional borrowings from the 15th edition for subjects not represented in the former.

[2] Pettee, J. *Subject headings* (New York, 1946), pp. 57–61.

[3] *Pace* Metcalfe, J. *Information indexing and subject cataloguing* (New York, 1957), pp. 147–149.

[4] Bliss, H. E. *Bibliographical classification*. Vol. 1 (New York, 1940).

[5] Ranganathan, S. R. *Classified catalogue code* (Madras, London, 1951), p. 174.

[6] See Bradford, S. C. *Documentation* (London, 1953), pp. 62–86.

[7] See Vickery, B. C. *Classification and indexing in science*. 2nd ed. (London, 1959), pp. 19–47.

# CHAPTER IX

## CHAIN PROCEDURE FOR SUBJECT INDEXES
## TO CLASSIFIED CATALOGUES

THE last chapter described how in the index to the Decimal Classification the order of the components of compound subjects is often the reverse of the order in which the same components appear as stages in the hierarchy of the classification scheme. For citation as parts of the subject index entry the components are given in specific-to-generic order. Thus, if

> Shorthand
>> English
>> Spanish

is part of the hierarchy of the classification scheme, the corresponding index entries are

> English shorthand
> Spanish shorthand
> Shorthand

No index Entry is given under 'Shorthand, English' or 'Shorthand, Spanish'.

Though in index entries the second term of the compound is the genus of the first term, it need not be the immediate genus. The classificatory hierarchy given above might well be more fully modulated as follows:

> Shorthand
>> Teutonic languages
>>> English
>> Romance languages
>>> Spanish

The subject index entries, however, remain unaltered. To insert the middle terms, as

| English | Teutonic languages | Shorthand |
| Spanish | Romance languages | Shorthand |

would add nothing to the concepts 'English Shorthand' and 'Spanish Shorthand'.

Although this method of indexing appeared first in the Index to the Decimal Classification, it is applied there rather hesitantly, and justified largely as an economy measure. Thus, the excerpt from the Decimal Classification Index under the heading 'Chemistry' quoted in the last chapter, included the entry 'Chemistry, Analytic'. It was left to S. R. Ranganathan to suggest that the method, under the name of 'chain procedure' should be applied rigorously as a systematic technique for subject-indexing a classified catalogue. Ranganathan had in mind its specific application to the Colon Classification, and, as part of our detailed examination of its effectiveness, we may begin by considering some examples of its use in connection with class symbols drawn from the Colon Classification.[1]

To produce the required subject index entries for the symbol NA561,J37,67:8 (meaning Model of the tower of a Tudor castle), we begin by writing down the meaning of each digit, beginning from the right, as follows:

| | |
|---|---|
| Model | 8 |
| Energy | : |
| Tower | 7 |
| Roof | 6 |
| Part | , |
| Castle | 7 |
| Dwelling | 3 |
| Tudor period | J |
| Period | , |
| England | I |
| Great Britain & Ireland | 6 |
| Europe | 5 |
| Architecture | A |
| Fine arts | N |

We notice at once that the terms corresponding to the punctuation digits are less concrete than the others.[2] This is because they represent connections between components rather than components themselves. Relationships always require the use of highly abstract terms (as we discovered in connection with Farradane's relational 'operators' in Chapter V). Terms of this kind are not sought by enquirers. These are designated by Ranganathan as a variety of 'False Link'. Since they are always represented in the Colon Classification notation by characteristic devices (punctuation symbols, and the digits 0 and 9), they declare themselves automatically. We therefore delete 'Energy', 'Part', and 'Period' from the list above.

The remaining words are the raw material of the subject index: they are the separate components which have now to be combined to form compound terms. The specific subject index entry will commence with the terms 'Model': the remaining words listed each introduce a generic subject index entry.

Let us rewrite the list, omitting the False Links, adding in front of the single digits on the right the preceding part of the composite symbol NA561,J37,67:8.

| | |
|---|---|
| Model | NA561,J37,67:8 |
| Tower | NA561,J37,67 |
| Roof | NA561,J37,6 |
| Castle | NA561,J37 |
| Dwelling | NA561,J3 |
| Tudor period | NA561,J |
| England | NA561 |
| Great Britain & Ireland | NA56 |
| Europe | NA5 |
| Architecture | NA |
| Fine arts | N |

It will be evident that apart from the last two, each of the above terms requires a qualifying subheading in order that it may correctly translate the symbol assigned to it. The subheadings needed for any term are drawn from the terms which follow it in the list. If more than one qualifying term is needed to specify the subject, the various terms must be given in the order of the list. We may now proceed to add qualifiers according to this rule.

| | |
|---|---|
| Model: Tower: Castle: Tudor period | NA561,J37,67: 8 |
| Tower: Castle: Tudor period | NA561,J37,67 |
| Roof: Castle: Tudor period | NA561,J37,6 |
| Castle: Tudor period: Architecture | NA561,J37 |
| Dwelling: Tudor period: Architecture | NA561,J3 |
| Tudor period: Architecture | NA561,J |
| England: Architecture | NA561 |
| Great Britain & Ireland: Architecture | NA56 |
| Europe: Architecture | NA5 |
| Architecture | NA |
| Fine arts | N |

It will be noticed that the first three terms do not require the qualifier 'Architecture'. As they relate to structural parts it may reasonably be assumed that reference is being made to architectural aspects. The entry 'Tudor period: Architecture' serves to draw attention to a further type of False Link which would not be wanted in the subject index. Had the castle concerned been of earlier date it could, for example, have been symbolised as NA561,G. The digit G here stands for the period 1200 to 1299 which has no name, and would therefore have to be treated as a False Link.

A further example from the Colon Classification may now be given. The symbol D663:21–96 means Protection of overhead direct current transmission lines from lightning. Proceeding as before, but partially telescoping the first two stages given in the earlier example, we have

| | |
|---|---|
| Lightning protection | D663 : 21–96 |
| Special problem | D663 : 21–9 |
| Application to | D663 : 21– |
| Overhead | D663 : 21 |
| Transmission | D663 : 2 |
| Energy | D663 : |
| Direct current | D663 |
| Electrical engineering | D66 |
| Mechanical engineering | D6 |
| Engineering | D |

Removing False Links and adding qualifiers, the following subject index entries are produced:

| | |
|---|---|
| Lightning protection: Overhead transmission: Direct current | D663 : 21–96 |
| Overhead transmission: Direct current | D663 : 21 |
| Transmission: Direct current | D663 : 2 |
| Direct current: Engineering | D663 |
| Electrical engineering | D66 |
| Mechanical engineering | D6 |
| Engineering | D |

The entry for Mechanical Engineering in this example calls for comment. Electrical Engineering is no longer regarded as a part of Mechanical Engineering and its appearance under that heading in the Colon Classification is an anachronism. The mechanical operation of chain procedure would result in serious misdirection of the catalogue user if the catalogue in fact contained no material on Mechanical Engineering. This illustrates one of the defects of the very virtues of chain procedure as used in conjunction with the Colon Classification. The very degree of mechanical correspondence between class symbol and entry which the expressive notation of the Colon Classification permits, does increase the danger that obvious faults in the classification may lead to false information in the subject index. Fortunately such faults are extremely rare in the Colon Classification.

The examples given above have shown the application of chain procedure to the indexing of compound subjects. Books which deal with the relationship between two subjects can equally be handled by the same method. For instance, the symbol R50gM2 (the Philosophy of Aesthetics as influenced by Journalism) produces chain procedure index entries as follows:

| | |
|---|---|
| Journalism – influencing Aesthetics, Philosophy | R50gM2 |
| Useful arts – influencing Aesthetics, Philosophy | R50gM |
| Aesthetics: Philosophy | R5 |
| Philosophy | R |

The connecting symbol 'og' (meaning 'influenced by') is treated as a False Link.

A slightly more complex situation may arise in indexing a work which compares two subjects. We may take as an illustration the symbol △63:60cQ6:4146 which is translated as Gnostic meditation compared with Christian prayer. Omitting the connecting symbol oc as in the previous example, together with other False Links, the following subject index entries are produced:

| | | |
|---|---|---|
| 1 | Prayer: Christianity – compared with Meditation, Gnosticism – | △63:360cQ6:4146 |
| 2 | Worship: Christianity – compared with Meditation, Gnosticism – | △63:360cQ6:414 |
| 3 | Personal Christianity – compared with Meditation, Gnosticism – | △63:360cQ6:41 |
| 4 | Practice, Christianity – compared with Meditation, Gnosticism – | △63:360cQ6:4 |
| 5 | Christianity – compared with Meditation, Gnosticism – | △63:360cQ6 |
| 6 | Religion – compared with Meditation, Gnosticism – | △63:360cQ |
| 7 | Meditation: Gnosticism | △63:36 |
| 8 | Technique: Gnosticism | △63:3 |
| 9 | Gnosticism | △63 |
| 10 | Christian mysticism | △6 |
| 11 | Mysticism | △ |

One point strikes us in reading this list. Items nos. 2 to 6 inclusive are not real subjects; literature is not to be found upon them, since comparison must always be between entities of the same order of magnitude. One might compare and contrast Christianity and Gnosticism, or Christian practice and Gnostic technique or Christian prayer and Gnostic meditation. Documents which compare or contrast two subjects do not therefore lend themselves to unmodified chain procedural indexing. It is, of course, not difficult to frame a general rule excluding the offending entries 2 to 6 above. We can establish as a practice the entry of the specific subject (no. 1 above) accompanied by normal chain procedure for the first subject compared only: or to put it in another way, after the specific subject entry, chain procedure is to be resumed only at the first digit to the left of the relational symbol 'o'. But this would mean that enquirers would be given no access to the material from the entry words Worship, Personal, Practice, Christianity, Religion. Of these, Worship, Christianity and Religion are essential approach words for which provision should somehow be made. (The question of the remaining two – Personal and Practice – will be put upon one side for the time being.)

The difficulty is resolved when we consider that every such instance of comparison between subjects requires two entries in the classified catalogue. When two subjects are compared (or contrasted) it is not possible to decide that one is more important or significant than the other. To classify the last example merely under Gnosticism is as arbitrary as it would be to classify it merely under Christianity. We must enter in both places in the classified catalogue. Our second entry will be under the symbol Q6:41460c△63:36, and the restricted chain procedure suggested in the last paragraph gives the following:

| | | |
|---|---|---|
| 12 | Meditation: Gnosticism – compared with | |
| | Prayer, Christianity – | Q6:41460c△63:36 |
| 13 | Prayer: Christianity | Q6:4146 |
| 14 | Worship: Christianity | Q6:414 |
| 15 | Personal Christianity | Q6:41 |
| 16 | Practice: Christianity | Q6:4 |
| 17 | Christianity | Q6 |
| 18 | Religion | Q |

The entries 14 to 18, it will be noticed, bring in precisely those entry words which were missing when the restricted chain procedure was applied to the earlier class symbol △63:360cQ6:4146. Reviewing the whole series 1 to 11, 12 to 18, we observe that Prayer and Meditation appear twice each as entry words. This suggests that the specific entries 1 and 12 are redundant. We are therefore left with the following rule: for composite symbols representing a comparative treatment of two subjects, make a second inverted entry in the classified catalogue, and make chain procedural subject entries merely from the symbols for the separate subjects.

It should perhaps be stressed that this special situation arises only when subjects are compared or contrasted. An example of influence or effect relationship has already been given. A further one is given to illustrate the need for giving *all* effective links in such cases.

| | |
|---|---|
| W6ogX723 – Democracy influenced by land tax | |
| Land: Taxes – influencing Democracy | W6ogX723 |
| Taxes – influencing Democracy | W6ogX72 |
| Public finance – influencing Democracy | W6ogX7 |
| Economics – influencing Democracy | W6ogX |
| Democracy | W6 |
| Political science | W |

Each of these entries represents a feasible subject upon which literature could appear, and each entry word represents a legitimate point of user access to the specific subject.

Similarly with the relationship between subjects designed by Ranganathan as 'Bias Phase' in which a subject is treated generally but from the point of view of a class of users whose primary interest lies in another subject. An example is EobM7:8 Chemistry for those primarily concerned with Textile Printing.

Chain procedure subject entries are:

| | |
|---|---|
| Printing: Textiles – Chemistry for | EobM7:8 |
| Textiles: Manufactures – Chemistry for | EobM7 |
| Manufactures – Chemistry for | EobM |
| Chemistry | E |

It remains to be added that Ranganathan, despite several restatements of the rules for chain procedure, applies the restricted chain procedure, similar to that envisaged on page 104 for comparison relationship to works exemplifying 'influence' relationship as well. The remedy involving double entry in the classified catalogue is, however, only available for comparison or contrast relationship, as the rules of the Colon Classification do not permit symbols to be constructed which would sanction double entry for influence or 'bias' relationship.

The three important claims made for chain procedure are first that it is economical compared with any alternative method, second that, apart from the fact that it gives no help in the discovery of synonyms, it is a mechanical method of subject indexing, and third that by the collocation of terms in the index it effectively signals subject relationships not expressed by collocation in the classified sequence of entries. In the remainder of this chapter we shall briefly consider each of these claims in turn, and finally go on to consider how the result of chain procedure, quite apart from these alleged advantages, meets the basic requirements of the user that the index entries produced should match

the terms in which he has, before approaching the catalogue, already
framed his enquiry.

### ECONOMY OF CHAIN PROCEDURE

On the question of economy some observations have been made in
the last chapter. Chain procedure is substantially more economical
than other possible systems because it eliminates permutation of components, so that for any particular compound subject, the saving is a
question of the ratio between the sum of the components and their
factorials. For terms of one or two components there is no saving; for
terms of three components (six permutations) there is a 50 per cent
saving in number of entries required: for terms of four components
(twenty-four possible permutations) there is a saving of 83.33 per cent,
and for longer compounds the economy is even greater. These figures
still, however, represent considerably less than the actual scale of the
economy gained. In a catalogue or index employing permutation we
have subject sequences such as

> GEOGRAPHY, Economic
> GEOGRAPHY, Historical
> GEOGRAPHY, Human
> GEOGRAPHY, Mathematical
> GEOGRAPHY, Political

and their inverses

> ECONOMIC GEOGRAPHY, etc.

It does not matter whether these are entries or references, or whether,
if references, they are in the form given above, or

> GEOGRAPHY     see also   ECONOMIC GEOGRAPHY
> GEOGRAPHY     see also   HISTORICAL GEOGRAPHY, etc.

In either case ten headings are needed to signify five subjects. In chain
procedure six entries suffice, one each for the five subjects under
Economic, Historical, Human, etc., and one further for Geography.
There can be little doubt that the claims made for economy of chain
procedure are justified.

### HOW FAR IS CHAIN PROCEDURE MECHANICAL?

The second claim made on behalf of chain procedure which we have
now to consider is that it provides a simple mechanical routine for
subject indexing. At the outset we may note the connection between
this claim and the preceding one. Permutative schemes of indexing are
rarely applied mechanically, because the result would be an index of

prohibitive size. There are, in fact, no subject cataloguing (or classification) systems in which full permutation is practiced. It is in the (economically) necessary modifications of mechanical permutation that much of the laboriously acquired and communicated 'art' of subject cataloguing may be said to reside.

It may have occurred to the reader that the selection of qualifier terms in subject index entries may not necessarily be an automatic process. In the examples given above, it happens that the lists produced by chain procedural analysis offer unequivocal sets of terms capable of completing the meaning of entry words. For each entry word there was only one term or set of terms in the list capable of serving as qualifier. It can, however, happen that the hierarchical list of terms offers two or more equally satisfactory ways of qualifying the entry word. Thus the index entry equivalent to the Colon Classification symbol X:516 could be

> Competition: Trade

or

> Competition: Economics

Both ways of citing the context in which the term 'Competition' is used are equally acceptable. Precisely because they are equally acceptable, the choice of qualifying term may be made subject to mechanical rule if desired. We could say, for instance, that when more than one generic term is capable of serving as qualifier, we would choose the hierarchically higher: we should thus index

> Competition: Economics
> Barter: Economics

rather than

> Competition: Trade
> Barter: Finance

So, though Ranganathan has not, in fact, laid down any rule for the choice of alternative qualifiers, the choice can be mechanically regulated.

In the examples already quoted, a further phenomenon has appeared, the handling of which seems to demand rather subtle discrimination on the part of the subject cataloguer. In discussing the needs of enquirer approach in the example on Gnosticism and Christianity, we selected some entry words thrown up by chain procedure as essential, thereby implying that some others were inessential. The terms which appeared probably redundant were 'Personal', 'Technique', and 'Practices'. Chain procedure does, in fact, generate a certain number of entry words which it seems unlikely that any enquirer will ever use as an approach term for any conceivable subject. Where a cataloguer is sure of their uselessness, he can, of course, delete them – but he will inevitably be confronted by borderline cases in which the right decision, whether to include or exclude them, will call for the acutest discriminative intuition. It would seem that the claim of chain procedure to be a mechanical operation fails on this point. Ranganathan has made several unsuccessful attempts to render these redundant terms logically captive. In the earliest statement of the rules of chain procedure, they are by implication included under the umbrella of False Links. We notice the designation "any Link of the Primary Phase having no special name". This would seem to identify the category of redundant terms, while begging the question as to what for practical purposes is meant by "special name". As a distinguishing phrase capable of being helpful on the practical level, this has as little value as Cutter's "established name". However, by the 3rd edition of the *Classified Catalogue Code* Ranganathan had redesignated these redundant terms as "Unsought Links" which he proceeded to treat as a separate category. This is a step toward clarification, since the False Links under which the redundant terms had formerly been included are identifiable in the Colon Classification by characteristic notation. An Unsought Link on the other hand is a manifestation, not of any factor within the classification but of the abstract or diffuse quality of the named concept itself. Unfortunately abstractness is not an absolute quality: there are degrees or graduations of abstractness and concreteness, and it is just this lack of a clear demarcation line which creates a difficulty for the subject cataloguer. We have here a problem, which, while not peculiar to chain procedure, is neither eliminated nor mechanically resolved by chain procedural technique. Ranganathan says that detailed decisions as to what are Unsought Links must depend upon the circumstances of the individual library concerned. At first glance this may seem a lame evasion, but it is rather more than that. Among the Unsought Links in the example illustrated above was

Technique: Gnosticism

It is fairly clear that this entry will be valueless in a general library or catalogue. It is, however, by no means certain that the entry is going to be useless in a library or catalogue of which the subject content is limited to religion. 'Technique', though possibly an unfamiliar word in the context, does stand for an aspect of religion upon which enquiries at this specialist library may perhaps be made. In other words it may not be Unsought. If we now go on to consider a library of yet narrower subject limitation, a library on mysticism, we can be sure that 'Technique' has now become a sought term, as the most cursory inspection of the literature on the subject will make clear.

Ranganathan in his latest statement on chain procedure[3] defines an Unsought Link as one which

> " (1) ends with a part of the Isolate Focus within a Facet of a Class Number;
> " (2) represents a subject on which reading material is not likely to be produced or sought or which is not likely to be looked up by any reader seeking materials on the Specific Subject forming the Last Link of the full Class Number".

The first part of this definition involves the omission from the index of certain of the generic terms produced by chain procedure. It is difficult to avoid altogether the suspicion that Ranganathan is here sacrificing certain substantial advantages accruing from chain procedure, in order to achieve some degree of mechanical control over Unsought Links. The second part of the definition is more easily understood. A subject 'on which reading Material is not likely to be produced" suggests one of Cutter's "unestablished subjects": and in the last part of the definition Ranganathan sacrifices some more generic entry words, having, one must assume, lost sight of the role of generic subject index entry in making possible the collective type of search in the classified catalogue.

The point of generic entry is not only that some readers may use it as a route to a more specific subject, but that someone may wish to collect all material within the generic field. Let us suppose that we index

Cows: Animal husbandry
Cows: Zoology
Ruminants: Zoology

omitting

Ruminants : Animal husbandry

on the incontestable ground that the stock farmer wanting material on cows would not look up 'Ruminants: Animal husbandry'. The result of the omission will, however, be that the enquirer wishing to review all material on Ruminants will miss the documents on domestic cows. We can justifiably omit any entry under Ruminants only if satisfied that this topic is never likely to be the subject of a collective enquiry.

On the whole we must conclude that the problem of Unsought Links still resists solution by formal rules.

Unsought Links can also appear as first qualifying terms immediately following the entry word. An example is X:957.73, which read backwards by chain procedure gives:

United States: Termination: Employment: Economics.

It is quite certain that neither in a general library nor in an economics library will the subject be sought under the caption 'United States: Termination . . .'; neither will any reader wish to collect material on Termination of everything under the sun in the United States. But from the practical viewpoint the situation is rather more satisfactory than when the Unsought term is entry word. In that case the issue is simply to omit or retain, and in resolving borderline cases of might-be-sought terms the cataloguer is forced to make agonising intuitive decisions. The question of omission does not arise when the qualifying term is an unsought one, as the entry word must remain. We cannot remove the unsought term from the qualifier section of the index entry, leaving

United States : Employment : Economics

for this does not correspond to the classification symbol X:957.73 but to X:95.73. All that we can do in such cases is to transpose the unsought term to a less important position in the index entry. This results in

United States : Employment : Termination : Economics  X : 957.73

Here we have the subject correctly stated, but the qualifying terms are not in the order given by chain procedure.

We have considered at some length certain situations arising in chain procedure which leave decisions – sometimes quite critical ones – to be made as best he can by the cataloguer : it is clear that the claim that chain procedure mechanises subject indexing must be a qualified one. It is, however, important to keep the question in correct perspective. Chain procedure does offer a methodical treatment of subject indexing far in advance of any alternative approach yet propounded : the points we have been considering are important, and await solution, but they are residual ones. On the whole, chain procedure is a considerable step towards mechanical subject indexing in a classified catalogue.

## EFFECTIVENESS OF CHAIN PROCEDURE

We now turn to a more fundamental question. To what extent is chain procedure efficient, first in terms of its ability to produce index names which match the subject names in the minds of enquirers, and second in terms of its ability to demonstrate subject relationships other than those embodied in the classification sequence or classified file?

In Chapter VI the relative importance or significance of the various component words in a compound subject designation was considered at some length. It was pointed out that the enquirer's choice of word for the purpose of consulting the catalogue was determined by the relative concreteness of the component words. Generally, the most concrete form (if there is one term in the compound name more concrete than all others) will be chosen as the starting point of the enquiry, though, as shown in column 4 of the Relationship Table (opposite p. 55), factors connected with the relations between components may sometimes modify this general rule. In the Colon Classification (and to a lesser extent in other schemes) the component symbols for composite subjects are similarly arranged in an order which commences with the most concrete concepts and finishes with the most abstract. For instance, the symbol D415,4:78 represents the three components Railroad, Gradient, Measurement arranged in concrete-to-abstract order. It will be obvious that when we come to chain index such a composite subject, using the normal reversal process, we shall produce index entries in which the entry word is more abstract than the word which follows it as qualifier. Our index entries for the above example would read

| | |
|---|---|
| Measurement : Gradients : Railroads | D415,4:78 |
| Construction : Gradients : Railroads | D415,4:7 |
| Gradients : Railroads : Engineering | D415,4 |
| Railroads : Engineering | D415 |

The first three index entries given here are in abstract-to-concrete order, and this would appear to be the case where ever the entry word and its qualifier belong to different facets. On the other hand when entry word and qualifier belong to the same facet or consist respectively of Personality Facet term and Main class term, as in the final index entry above, the order concrete-to-abstract would seem to be usual.

It is a legitimate criticism of chain procedure that the specific entry for the subject given above is likely to be formulated by the enquirer as 'Railroads, Gradients, Measurements', and that the subject, though so represented in the classified file, does not appear in this form in the subject index. The enquirer is, of course, given access to his material by means of a subject index entry under his first word 'Railroads'. This will take him to the classified file at D415, at which area, with the help of the classificatory layout of subjects and the supporting feature headings, he will locate 'Gradients, Measurement' without difficulty. In point of helpfulness the generic entry falls short of the specific type of concrete-to-abstract index heading in two ways. The specific subject required may not be represented in the catalogue, but this fact is not revealed in the subject index : it is discovered only at the end of a fruitless search in the classified file. Secondly, the entry 'Railroads, Engineering' may not be the only one under 'Railroads' in the index. The enquirer is then left with the task of allocating the concept 'Gradients, Measurement' to one of a number of qualifying subheadings. This may not always be easy, especially as generic class terms often have a more restricted connotation in popular usage than that employed by the classification maker. We are bound to conclude that chain procedure does erect certain obstacles (albeit surmountable ones) to the enquirer who has formulated his subject specifically. These are inherent in the system and there is no ameliorating action that can be taken. The difficulty should not, of course, exist for professional staff using the catalogue, who can be trained to look up composite subjects in abstract-to-concrete order of component citation. Other users cannot be expected to learn the rationale of the system, but much difficulty due to conditioning derived from other types of indexes might be avoided if ways can be found of impressing upon enquirers that chain procedure subject entries are generic as well as specific signposts to material.

The final question which we set outselves to answer in this chapter is how far the chain procedure index succeeds by alphabetical collocation of entries on related subjects in showing those subject relationships which are not expressed in the classified sequence. The general answer must be that chain procedure succeeds in this better than less systematised methods of indexing, because to cite the hierarchy of generic concepts which comprise a given specific concept is virtually to analyse the latter into its elementary constituent ideas. Accidental subject collocation in alphabetical indexes normally shows subject relationship in only a limited fashion because the words used are generally complexes of more elementary concepts. Only the complex term is indexed and not the elementary terms which logically underlie it. When we say that two subjects are related, we mean that they share some common elementary concept or concepts. It is clear that if it were practicable to denote all subjects in an alphabetical index, not by single terms representing complexes of elementary concepts, but by strings of the elementary concepts themselves (fully permuted in a non-chain procedural index), then all relationships between subjects would be brought out by alphabetical collocation. We may remind ourselves again of the already quoted

> Labour, Costs
> Labour, Disputes

which shows relationship by collocation, and

> Wages
> Labour, Disputes

which does not.

Among the Canons of Classification set forth by W. C. B. Sayers is to be found the assertion that the hierarchy of classificatory terms should be fully modulated. The genus of any term should be its immediate genus. The classification schedule, should, in other words, omit no step in the hierarchy. We should for instance have

> Music
>> Instrumental
>>> Stringed
>>>> Plucked
>>>>> Lute

rather than

> Music
>> Instrumental
>>> Lute

or

> Music
>> Stringed instruments
>>> Lute

Few classification schemes have attempted a consistent application of this principle, though the Colon Scheme has gone further in this direction than the others. However, even in the Colon Scheme it is not difficult to find examples of omitted generic terms. Thus, under M3 Domestic Science we have direct division to M31 and M32, Cookery and Sewing respectively. The chain procedure gives no access to Cookery from Food, and the list of relationships connected with Food in the subject index is to that extent lacking in comprehensiveness.

In enumerating the more detailed particulars, all general classifications tend to omit generic terms representing properties at the lowest stages of the hierarchy. In the Colon Classification such omission is often the result of Favoured Category mechanism, which removes a subject from its logical position and places it in a forward location. Another common reason for the omission of intermediate stages of the hierarchy is lack of literary warrant. This in 2 Library Science we have special classes of library users enumerated as

263  Prisoner
264  Hospital

The index entries for 263 and 264 fail to provide approaches from Criminology and Medicine or Diseases, presumably because there is no literary warrant for Libraries for Criminals or Libraries for the Sick. Theoretically it should be possible, and in documentation work may be desirable, to designate a place for every topic in such a way that its properties appear as genera at various levels, so that subject index collocation would cover all possible relationships.

We may attempt a brief résumé of our survey of chain procedure in its intended field of application, a catalogue classified by the Colon Classification. Its importance lies in the fact that it is the first systematic procedure laid down for subject indexing. It is nearly, though not quite, mechanical in its method of working. It scores heavily over earlier practices on grounds of economy. It provides entry word approach for compound subjects through a combined system of generic and specific entries; but it has the disadvantage that the components in its compound subject entries are not given in the order in which most enquirers will think of them. Finally, it demonstrates subject relationship by alphabetical collocation of entries on different aspects of the same subject. It is limited in this respect only by the extent to which the Colon Classification fails to 'modulate' fully in the listing of terms in hierarchy.

## NOTES AND REFERENCES

[1] The class symbols used in this chapter are taken from the 5th edition of the *Colon Classification* (Madras, London, 1957).
[2] See Ranganathan, S. R. *Colon Classification* (Madras, London, 1957), p. 161.
[3] Ranganathan, S. R. *Classified catalogue code* (Madras, London, 1958), p. 323.

CHAPTER X

# CHAIN PROCEDURE APPLIED TO THE
# DECIMAL CLASSIFICATION[1]

SYMBOLS for any scheme of classification can be used as the basis for
chain procedural subject indexing.[2] A class number such as 331.283
from the Decimal Classification can be treated in the same manner as
the Colon Classification symbols used as examples in the last chapter.

| | |
|---|---|
| Agriculture | 3 |
| Special industries | 8 |
| Wages | 2 |
| Labour | 1 |
| Economics | 3 |
| Social sciences | 3 |

The second term in this list is a False Link, but there is no characteristic False Link digit to warn us of the fact such as we find in the Colon
Classification. Omitting this term and adding qualifiers, we produce
the following entries :

| | |
|---|---|
| Agriculture : Wages : Economics | 331.283 |
| Wages : Economics | 331.2 |
| Labour : Economics | 331 |
| Economics | 330 |
| Social sciences | 300 |

It is sometimes said that chain procedural indexing cannot be better
than the scheme to which it is applied. This is true for the major con-
structional faults in a scheme. These will tend to produce groups of
index entries containing the same entry word distinguished by
qualifiers which are nearly equivalent or only very subtly differentiated. For instance

| | |
|---|---|
| Christmas : Holidays : Social customs | 394.268[1] |
| Christmas : Folklore | 398.33241 |
| | |
| France : Economic conditions | 330.944 |
| France : Economic organisation | 338.0944 |
| France : Economic planning | 338.944 |

As a general rule, the better the classification scheme, the fewer will be the number of highly generalised terms, such as 'organisation' above, which will be required in the qualifier sections of entries. However, mistakes and omissions in the schedule, due to oversight or merely slipshod thinking can, if detected by the subject cataloguer, to a great extent be made good by chain procedure. Just because of this corrective role, chain procedure applied to a less logically coherent scheme is bound to be less mechanical in operation than when applied to the Colon scheme.

Whereas in chain procedural indexing to the Colon scheme, the subject indexer can virtually limit the field of his concern to the digits of the notation, in applying the technique to the Decimal Classification he must maintain a close watch on the classification schedule of terms as well. This critical appraisal of the classification schedule may at first sight seem to involve a great deal of work for the subject indexer : but it is actually the work which the classifier must perform in order to classify. So that if classification and subject indexing are carried out as a unitary operation, there will be no superfluity of effort. In fact, chain procedure is an excellent and necessary check on the possibility of the classifier's jumping of mental fences out of turn.

Two levels of critical examination of the classification scheme are required.

### NON-HIERARCHICAL NOTATION IN THE DECIMAL CLASSIFICATION

In the first place the indexer has to consider the relation between the notation and the structure of the scheme. A notation is primarily a means of mechanising the order of terms in a systematic sequence. It need not necessarily reflect the hierarchical relations between terms, and in the Decimal Classification it often does not. So it is insufficient merely to rely on the digits of the Decimal Classification class number to produce all necessary entry words. Thus D.C. symbol 227 produces

> Epistles : Bible        227
> Bible                   220

Something has obviously been omitted here; and a glance at the schedules confirms that there is an intermediate term generic to Epistles and subordinate to Bible. This is New Testament, but it has the notation 225. The fact that this term is required for indexing cannot be inferred from inspection of class number 227 alone. It may be asked how one can subject index to 225 in this case when the catalogue may contain no material classified at this number? The answer is that in such a case a guide card must be inserted at 225. Generic entries in the subject index may or may not have entries for material at the generic class number in the classified file. If there are no entries in the classified file, the generic subject index entry refers to a guide in the classified file.

A useful, though, as the above example shows, not an invariable indication that the hierarchy is not reflected in notation is given when the schedule caption at a particular number consists of two or more names which are not synonyms. Thus in setting down the chain of terms applicable to 575 Evolution, the removal of the last digit leaves us with

570　Archeology. Biology

This is of some assistance in reminding us that the generic term required is Biology, and the indexer's next step is to search the schedule between 570 and 575 for the specific place for Biology. This is to be found in slightly disguised terms (in the 14th edition of the D.C.) at 574. Entries required are therefore

Evolution　　575
Biology　　　574

It can happen that a required generic term listed in the schedule as part of a combined caption is given no precise class number though symbols are assigned for its subdivisions. An example in D.C. is Printing which appears as

655　Printing, Book Trade

This caption is immediately followed by class numbers for the subdivisions of Printing. A possible method of dealing with this situation is to be found in the use of the [1] device employed by the *British National Bibliography* and described later in this chapter.

In the examples given above, the indexer has been obliged to supply additional indexing terms other than those which would be indicated automatically by hierarchical notation. The notation can on occasion operate in the opposite sense by suggesting for inclusion a term which is not a true genus of the specific subject concerned. Thus, if we remove the final digit from 658.8 Selling, we are left with 658 Management. Selling is, of course, not a part of Management but of the wider concept Business. The indexer must not allow the non-hierarchical notation to beguile him into indexing an irrelevant term.

### DECIMAL CLASSIFICATION STRUCTURE AND CHAIN
#### PROCEDURE

The pitfalls so far noted can be avoided by not relying upon notation to signal hierarchical relationships. The class of problems now to be considered arises from omissions and errors in the classification schedule itself. These must at least be mentally corrected by the subject indexer, otherwise the subject index will prove inadequate.

A fairly common difficulty in chain indexing from D.C. arises from incomplete modulation of terms in hierarchy. Details may be scheduled but the overlying concept which embraces them all is not mentioned. If we have to chain index 251 Preaching, we analyse as follows :

| | |
|---|---|
| Preaching | 251 |
| Pastoral work | 250 |
| Religion | 200 |

There are two terms missing between Pastoral work and Religion. They are not mentioned in the schedule, though they may be inferred from a careful scrutiny of the classificatory layout. An adequate set of entries for the above example would be

| | |
|---|---|
| Preaching | 251 |
| Pastoral work : Church : Christianity | 250 |
| Church : Christianity | 250/280 |
| Christianity | 220/280 |
| Religion | 200 |

In this case by using a conventional sign meaning 'to' (or 'through' in American English), we have indexed terms which have no specific numbers in the D.C. Comparable examples are the following :

| | |
|---|---|
| Inland water transport : Economics | 386 |
| Water transport : Economics | 386/387.5 |
| Transport : Economics | 385/388 |
| Commerce : Economics | 380 |
| Canals : Engineering | 626 |
| Hydraulic engineering | 626/627 |
| Civil engineering | 624/628 |
| Engineering | 620 |

A necessary intermediate generic term may not be missing but wrongly displaced to another part of the schedule. Thus the first of the two examples given above falls within the field of Economics but pure chain procedure produces no entry under that term because Economics at 330 is wrongly separated from Commerce (which is one of its main divisions) by alien material. We cannot proceed as we did with Biology and Evolution above. An index entry to 330 would in no sense be a signpost to 380 because Law, Public Administration and Social Welfare are interposed between them. We must therefore supplement our chain procedure by a connective index entry as follows :

    Economics : Commerce                380

It will be noted that this permutes a chain procedure entry already supplied.

One further problem connected with indexing derived from classification schedules remains to be mentioned. This is that the schedules may not be sufficiently detailed to permit specific classification of the material concerned. Thus the topic British Divorce Law has no specific place in 14th edition D.C. The generic heading closest to it which has notation is 347.6 British Family Law. But it will not be very satisfactory to index

    Divorce : British law                 347.6

since the class number 347.6 in the classified file will also contain material on such topics as Family Law, Inheritance, Intestacy, Marriage Law. In other words the direction to the enquirer to go to 347.6, though correct as far as it goes, is inexact. Having arrived at 347.6 he has, if he wishes to survey all available material on British Divorce Law, to examine a large number of individual titles most of which will be on other subjects. A partial solution to this problem will be noticed shortly in the description of chain indexing practice by the *British National Bibliography*.

### BRITISH NATIONAL BIBLIOGRAPHY SUBJECT INDEXING

It is well known that a large scale application of chain procedure to the Decimal Classification is made in the *British National Bibliography*. It was adopted there after a year of experiment and in the face of some initial scepticism on the part of the writer. Its economy in operation and in terms of number of entries required were qualities likely to commend themselves to an enterprise working upon small financial margins, but a more important reason for its adoption by the *B.N.B.* lay in the need for exceptional speed of decision in subject indexing and classification matters. The *B.N.B.* publishes at weekly intervals a current classified bibliography of the total output of British publishing (apart from periodicals and a few minor excluded categories of material). These two factors, the brief publication interval and the anticipated volume of material (at the time of writing about 375 items per week), combined to create a problem in the control of the classification and subject indexing process which is probably of unparalleled severity. A work intake of this size can be classified to produce a fully coherent pattern, provided that the person with ultimate responsibility can be allowed a certain time-lag between tentative and finalised decisions. More generally, however complex and voluminous the material, it is possible by feeling one's way and proceeding empirically to attain the optimum arrangement possible with the classification scheme in use and also to compile an effective subject index; provided that time can be allowed for comparing late decisions with early ones and making adjustments as required. Owing to the publication programme, tentative decisions could have no place in B.N.B. practice. Final decisions were required immediately for weekly publication. Slightly more latitude is theoretically available for subject index decisions (the subject index is published monthly), but to take advantage of this, it would have been necessary to set up a separate subject index department. For reasons of economy and because it was felt to be inherently undesirable that two basically similar intellectual operations should be performed twice over by different people, this was not done.

The problem was therefore to find ways of reducing to a minimum the area of free decision left to the chief subject cataloguer in order that he should not be swamped by the demand for instant, final and largely irrevocable decisions, which might constitute precedents for the analogous handling of new subjects at present unforeseen.

Fortunately two techniques were available which would help in this situation. Facet analysis made it possible to lay down a comprehensive ground plan, which, once adopted, eliminated the need for further decisions on a wide range of practical issues in classification. Similarly, chain procedure set a pattern for subject indexing method which disposed of the need for individual determination of every vexatious question of component order and permutation. The chief subject cataloguer was thus free to attend to those residual questions which cannot be resolved by any rule or pattern of practice. An important incidental advantage of chain procedure was that subordinate staff could be instructed very rapidly, and once familiar with the method, they had the satisfaction of working to a plan which they could understand rather than to the inscrutable edicts of someone in authority.

The use of chain procedure by B.N.B. required the acceptance of two concomitant conditions. These were first, that some means should be found of classifying specifically, irrespective of whether the Decimal Classification provided specific notation for the topic concerned or otherwise; and second, that every entry in the classified file should include a heading which stated the subject in words.

The reasons for these conditions will be readily understood. A subject index confined to the terms which are given specific notation by the Decimal Classification would have been quite inadequate. Subject headings were needed for the classified entries to compensate for the lack of permutation in the index. Thus an enquirer seeking material on Aircraft Engines and finding in the index under Aircraft only the generic entry 'Aircraft : Engineering 629.13' and turning to 629.13 in the classified file, would require the classified layout under that heading to be clearly displayed in words. This is in any case desirable on general grounds. It is one of the surprising features of most pre-*B.N.B.* catalogues that a sequence of D.C. symbols, uninterpreted except at intervals for general guide cards, was felt to be self-explanatory for enquirers.

It proved possible to meet both of these needs by means of a single mechanism. All D.C. class numbers used in the classified file are translated into words, the translation forming what has come to be known as a 'Feature Heading'. Thus the entries for material on Aircraft Engines are preceded by the combined class symbol and feature heading

629.13      –   ENGINES.

It is to be noted that the feature heading translates, not the whole class symbol, but merely its last element. Its import is clear when read in context with higher terms in the hierarchy.

629.13      –   AIRCRAFT
629.1343    –   PARTS OF AIRCRAFT
629.13435   –   ENGINES

The generic terms appear in the bibliography either as feature headings to entries on generic subjects, or, if there are no entries, as guides to the subject arrangement.

For books on subjects with no specific D.C. notation, the device [1] is added to the D.C. class number for the nearest containing head. After the [1] the name of the specific subject is added as a feature heading, e.g.,

629.13435[1]  –  GAS TURBINES

Provision of feature headings after [1] may be carried any number of stages that may be necessary for specification, e.g.,

> 629.13435[1]   –   GAS TURBINES. AIR INTAKES. DIMENSIONS

Chain procedure indexing is carried out by citing each of these terms, with necessary qualifiers, just as if they possessed specific notation. By this device entries on topics without specific notation are grouped together, separated both from other unspecified topics placed at the same D.C. number, and also from the more general material which the notation specifies, e.g.,

> 629.13435        –   ENGINES
> 629.13435[1]    –   COOLING SYSTEMS
> 629.13435[1]    –   GAS TURBINES

The actual form of the device [1] was not quite arbitrarily chosen. It was found that in the majority of instances in which the D.C. had been content with partial development, the missing subjects belonged to positions before the first scheduled division. They therefore needed to be represented by a device which sorted before the digit 1 (but after 099). Hence the pair of brackets have an anteriorising function : they place the symbol [1] into a forward position ahead of 1 without brackets.

The [1] with verbal extension has on the whole proved a fairly satisfactory substitute for a fully developed notation. It is not, however, without problems, both for the cataloguer and for the enquirer. From the cataloguer it demands the task of classification schedule construction, sometimes at a specialised level. His background of facet analysis is of great assistance here, but it does not save him from one pitfall to which classification makers are always prone – the failure to modulate in hierarchy. Thus for oxy-acetylene welding of pipelines one is tempted to write

> 621.8672[1]    –   PIPELINES. WELDING. OXY-ACETYLENE
>                          WELDING

omitting to make provision for the important approach term Gas welding, which is then also omitted from the subject index. In a fully modulated feature heading it appears as follows :

> 621.8672[1]    –   PIPELINES. WELDING. GAS WELDING. OXY-
>                          ACETYLENE WELDING.

The difficulty arising from verbal substitutes for specific notation which affects the enquirer is that particular topics specified verbally after the same class number have no ordinal relationship with one another. They can, of course, be sorted alphabetically, but this usually gives a jumble, except where they all belong to the same category of division. Alphabetical arrangement of the verbal extensions used by B.N.B. after 622.33 [1] gives the following sequence

| | | |
|---|---|---|
| 622.33 | – | COAL MINES |
| 622.33[1] | – | EQUIPMENT |
| | | LIGHTING |
| | | PROSPECTING |
| | | ROOFS |
| | | SAFETY |
| | | SHOTFIRING |
| | | SURVEYING |
| | | TRANSPORT |

This is inadmissible in a sequence which purports to be classified. Their actual arrangement in *B.N.B.* is as follows :

| | | |
|---|---|---|
| 622.33 | – | COAL MINES |
| 622.33[1] | – | SAFETY |
| | | PROSPECTING |
| | | SURVEYING |
| | | EQUIPMENT |
| | | LIGHTING |
| | | ROOFS |
| | | SHOTFIRING |
| | | TRANSPORT |

The lack of ordinal value attaching to the verbal extensions after [1] becomes something of a burden to the catalogue user when the number of separately specified topics under the same class number is large. The subject index entry in such cases gives only an approximate location of the desired subject.

The uncertain dividing line between sought and unsought terms remains a matter of difficulty, irrespective of the classification scheme to which chain procedure is being applied. It is particularly hard to determine for a catalogue of general scope, and remains the most intractable of all subject cataloguing problems at *B.N.B.* Though it has not been possible to formulate any systematic solution, some description of the practice on this point may be of interest.

Terms denoting Form Divisions, such as Encyclopaedias, Periodicals, Tables and the like have been treated as Unsought Links, because it is felt that they would be used insufficiently to justify the large increase in entries which they would produce in the subject index.

Much more difficult problems are met in connection with a further group of subject terms of very wide connotation often treated as common subdivisions in classification schemes. Examples are Societies, Law, Organisation, Nomenclature, Classification, Analysis, Finance, Repairs, Servicing, Equipment, Theory, Psychology, Technique, Preservation, Specifications, Training, Safety. All of these terms can be applied to a wide variety of more concrete subjects and some of them would be quite out of place as entry words in a general subject catalogue. For example, such a series as

Technique : Architecture
Technique : Ballet
Technique : Casting : Metals
Technique : Diving
Technique : Engraving

would make no sense in a general subject index:[3] no user is likely to wish to collect material on Techniques as a whole. Lack of significance for a collective type of enquiry is a useful criterion for determining whether a term should be treated as Unsought. With Technique, we may group Societies, Organisation, Nomenclature, Repairs, Servicing, Equipment and Theory. No one consulting a general subject index will wish to collect documents on all aspects of any of these terms, even though in the case of Societies and Organisation there is Literature on them generally. The term Safety, particularly Industrial Safety, denotes a definite field of study, and the index must make provision for collective enquiries covering, if not the total field, at least wide portions of it. Therefore, Safety, occurring in whatever connection, is always indexed as a sought term. The same may be said of Psychology. The terms Analysis and Finance create a more complicated situation. No one will make an enquiry for all aspects of Analysis, but analytical chemists may wish to collect all references to Analysis which mean chemical analysis. The term also has a technical meaning in such fields as Mathematics and Physics of Sound. The practice of *B.N.B.* is therefore to index analysis as a sought term when (a) it means chemical analysis, (b) it has a special technical meaning. In other cases it is treated as an unsought term. Finance is rather more difficult to treat with any consistency. The financial aspect of practically any activity can be the subject of literature and it is reasonably certain that no one would wish to collect it all. However, there are certain definite fields in which Finance might well be the subject of a collective enquiry; one might enumerate Business Management, Home economics, and Public Administration. Finance is treated by *B.N.B.* as a sought term when it occurs within these fields, but some difficult questions remain. Is any economist ever going to require all material on the financial aspects of every industry? No certain answer is possible. The *B.N.B.* treats Finance in this last instance as an unsought term, but the grounds for doing so are admittedly hazardous. Many other examples exist of dubiously unsought terms upon which questionable decisions have perforce been made.

As was explained in the last chapter, Unsought Links arising in the qualifier section of the subject index entry can usually be transposed to a later position in the entry. The following examples illustrate this practice :

| | |
|---|---|
| Navigation : Ship equipment | 623.86[1] |
| Transport : Military administration | 355.69[1] |
| United States : Social organisation | 301.40973 |

Under unmodified chain procedure the final term of each of the above would be the first qualifier, thus

Navigation : Equipment : Ships
Transport : Administration : Military forces
United States : Organisation : Society

It will be noticed that the transposition of the qualifier terms has in these examples also involved the combination of the separate terms into single adjective-noun phrases. Transposition and combination of separate words in the qualifier section into phrases has also been employed for the purpose of reducing the number of stages of subheadings required for qualification. There is some evidence that intelligibility of the index entries is diminished if more than two stages of qualifying subheadings are used after the entry word. Thus, to retain the limitation to two stages, the entry

Coal : Mining : Planning : Economics

is modified to

Coal : Mining : Economic planning

Transposition and combination of qualifier words into phrase form is a practice which needs to be used with circumspection, as it can give rise to anomalies when subject entries are sorted together. Thus, one might be tempted to modify

Lighting : Plant : Wool manufactures : Economics

to

Lighting : Wool manufacturing plant : Economics

A work upon the technical rather than the economic aspects of the same problem would be entered as

> Lighting : Plant : Wool manufactures

and as there are only two stages of qualification here, there would be no occasion for transposing terms. However,

> : Plant : Wool manufactures

and

> : Wool manufacturing plant

cannot be tolerated as subheadings to the same entry word. If identical sets of qualifier terms appear twice or more often after the same entry word, they must be cited in the same form and order.

We may appropriately pass at this juncture to consider some more general aspects of the form of the subject index index entries in the B.N.B. With some exceptions to be noted later, the entry words are plural substantives. It would often be possible to give the entry word and first qualifier term as a single adjective-noun or noun-noun phrase. We might, for instance, without contravening the essence of the chain procedural method, give

> Financial economics            332

instead of

> Finance : Economics            332

Some general advantages of the subheaded form of entry over the phrase form have already been given in Chapter III (p. 23). In a combined author-title-subject index sequence such as the B.N.B. alphabetical index, it is particularly necessary to ensure that the same concept is not represented sometimes by a noun and at other times at some distance in the sequence by an adjective in an adjective-noun phrase. If this ambiguity is permitted, the efficiency of the index in dealing with both specific and collective enquiries will be impaired.

Noun-noun phrases, such as University Libraries, can usually be split into

> Universities : Libraries

without becoming unintelligible or ambiguous. Similarly, adjective-noun phrases in which the adjective is the equivalent of a concrete noun, can be rendered by two nouns. E.g., Solar Interference of Telecommunication is given as

> Sun : Interference : Telecommunications

Compound subjects of the types numbered 8 to 19 in the Relationship Table (opposite p. 55) may often require index entry in the phrase form rather than in that using separated substantives. In these cases, a particular variety of thing, product or action is designated by means of the name of a part, material, or principle of action. The use of adjectival phrase or substantive form depends upon whether the part, material or, principle of action can also be applied to other varieties of the thing, product or action. Thus Evaporation of Milk is a process not limited to the variety of milk called Evaporated Milk.[4] Therefore, for the process itself we retain the substantive form

Evaporation : Milk

but for the product, the adjectival phrase form is used.

Evaporated milk

A work dealing with the evaporation process in the production of evaporated milk would be classified under the product Evaporated Milk, and as this phrase is indexed at the generic level, Evaporation can be treated as an unsought term in this case.

To illustrate the reverse situation, we may take Lead Sheathed Cables. Any documents on the Lead used or the Lead Sheath will relate exclusively to the variety of cables known as Lead Sheathed Cables. The index form

Lead : Sheaths : Cables

is therefore used to denote Lead Sheathed Cables, and to cover the subordinate idea of the Lead of Lead Sheathed Cables, which is treated as an unsought term.

Established phrases include as part of their meaning the relationship between the components. Their replacement in the index by substantives might therefore appear to result in some diminution of clarity in index entries. In Chapter III it was pointed out that index language can nearly always dispense with relational words, because the kind of relationship can usually be inferred from the mere juxtaposition of the terms for the concepts related. This has been generally true for the subject index entries used in *B.N.B.* Groups of terms placed together without benefit· of connective relational words are almost always logically capable of plural interpretation, but in most cases there is an overwhelming literary or conventional warrant for one particular interpretation over all others. The fact just noted that phrases consisting of juxtaposed terms are used to convey unambiguous meanings is indirect evidence of this. Thus the phrase 'Photographic Chemistry' means unequivocally those chemical phenomena and operations pertaining to the practice of photography. Logically it could also mean photographic methods in practical chemistry, but in fact it is never understood as such. *B.N.B.* practice reflects the view that the components of such a phrase retain their fixed meaning even when the adjectival component is rendered as a noun and irrespective of the order of citation. Thus, it is assumed that the entry

Chemistry : Photography

bears the same unequivocal meaning as 'Photographic chemistry'. One point may be added. The entry need not be self-explanatory in the sense that it should enlighten someone who does not know the meaning of 'Photographic chemistry'. This example is included among several quoted by J. Metcalfe in an attack upon chain procedure.[5] His other examples are rather far-fetched. He thinks that

Photography : Careers

might mean Photographs of Careers, and

Photography : Bibliographies

could be 'photographs as a specification of Bibliography'. However, Metcalfe has put his finger upon one of the fundamental problems of indexing, even if he is indifferently served by his examples. Literary and conventional warrant for a particular interpretation is a fortunate accident which cover all but a minute fraction of the *B.N.B.* subject index entries. This fraction would, however, be rather larger for an index containing more complex combinations of concepts, and, although quantitatively insignificant for *B.N.B.*, merits close attention on more general grounds.

Ambiguity can often be reduced by careful selection and ordering of qualifier terms. Thus the entry

Owls : Control : Pests : Agriculture

could mean the control of owls necessitated by the damage they do to agriculture : or it could mean the control of agricultural pests *by* owls. If we wish to convey the second meaning, we can say

Owls : Biological control : Pests : Agriculture

or

Owls : Control agents : Pests : Agriculture

For the first of these two solutions we have merely made use of an intermediate term in the chain, which at first sight seemed unnecessary. The second solution, which is the better one, introduces the word 'agents', the function of which is to express the relationship between owls and control. As has been stressed above, the alternative interpretation is never absolutely ruled out. The solutions suggested above are not foolproof, but if we can contrive that the entry word and its first qualifier are in the simplest relationships, namely the appositional relationship, requiring that the first colon be translated 'as' in natural language, or part of the verb 'to be' in the language of statements. (Owls *as* Control agents, or Owls *are* Control agents), enquirers will normally interpret the entry in the sense intended.

The method of amplifying qualifiers suggested here is not always applicable. The entry

Library economy : Bibliographies          016.02

could mean either the use of bibliographies in library economy, or the bibliography of library economy. No amount of manipulation of qualifier terms will help in this instance. The matter can only be clarified by adding a preposition.

Library economy : Bibliographies of

This example illustrates a further interesting point. A high proportion of cases in which ambiguity arises in the chain procedure are those in which part of the class symbol is built up according to the direction 'divide like the whole classification'.

As pointed out in the last chapter, the components of compound subject terms normally appear in the abstract-concrete order as a result of chain procedure, the concrete term being indexed as the entry word of a generic concept. Thus we have

| | |
|---|---|
| Business methods | 650 |
| Correspondence : Business | 651.7 |
| English language : Business | 651.7[I] |
| Management : Business | 658 |
| Personnel : Business | 658.3 |

but not

| | |
|---|---|
| Business : Correspondence | 651.7 |
| Business English | 651.74 |
| Business management | 658 |
| Business : Personnel | 658.3 |

The desirability of citing components in concrete-abstract order in the alphabetico-specific catalogue has already been stressed in Chapter V. The absence of this order in subject index entries must be acknowledged to be a disadvantage of chain procedure, though not a critical one, because the concrete-abstract order of citation is in fact found in the classified file. All classified catalogues require the reader to make a two-stage reference to find what material is available on a given subject: if chain procedure is used, he is also required to make a two-stage reference to discover if a certain topic, formulated in concrete-abstract order, is represented at all. This is the price which chain procedure exacts for its solution of the problem of permutation of components. In applying chain procedure to the Decimal Classification, the abstract-concrete order of components does not emerge in subject index entries as consistently as in the case of the Colon Classification. Faults in the D.C. structure sometimes rather surprisingly produce subject index entries in concrete-abstract order. In one further situation *B.N.B.* produces entries in concrete-abstract order which are also contrary to chain procedure order. This is where in established phrases the concrete term is so wide in connotation that the compound subject may not be easily located in the classified file. Thus, for instance, phrases beginning with the term 'Social' are indexed as they stand in what may be termed 'anti-chain procedural order'. Under strict chain procedure, the subjects concerned would be indexed as

| | |
|---|---|
| Social sciences | 300 |
| Welfare : Social sciences | 360 |
| Psychology : Social sciences | 301.15 |
| Planning : Social sciences | 309.2 |
| Surveys : Social sciences | 309.1 |

In the *B.N.B.* subject index, the above are permuted in phrase form

| | |
|---|---|
| Social sciences | 300 |
| Social welfare | 360 |
| Social psychology | 301.15 |
| Social planning | 309.2 |
| Social surveys | 309.1 |

Situations such as this are, however, comparatively rare in *B.N.B.* practice.

The final question considered in the last chapter must now be taken up again in connection with the Decimal Classification. How comprehensively do the collocated subject index entries indicate subject relationships not expressed in the classified file? It seems probable that the *B.N.B.* subject index is somewhat inferior in this respect to one which would be derived from classification of the same material by the Colon scheme. This is because the D.C. schedules are less governed by rigorous analysis than are those of the Colon scheme. In particular, hierarchical modulation is often imperfect. The practice of isolating important subjects from their logical contexts, called in the Colon Classification the Favoured Category Device, is also in evidence in the Decimal Classification. Though this is justified on general grounds of ease of enquirer access, it is inimical to the relating power of the chain index. In the Decimal Classification we have

India : Religions                               299.11

but, on Favoured Category principles, Hinduism, the dominant religion of that country is set apart at 294.5, along with Vedic religion and its other derivatives. Whenever such a situation is recognised, *B.N.B.* makes a connective subject index entry

India : Hinduism                             294.5

If a brief summing up of *B.N.B.* experience in the application of chain procedure to a general classification scheme of traditional type may now be attempted, it may be said that once provision has been made for the isolation of unscheduled topics and provided that the subject cataloguer is trained to base his analysis upon the schedule rather than upon notation, the method works with very little more difficulty than when used as originally intended with the Colon Classification. Gross errors of modulation in the scheme do affect the index, but, once detected, the omission can be made good by connective index entries of the type illustrated in the preceding paragraph. Errors of facet order in the classification scheme do not in themselves result in the omission of important approach terms from the index. They may, however, produce sets of entries, in which the same entry word is variously qualified with an unfortunate degree of subtlety, as in the example quoted earlier

France : Economic conditions          330.944
France : Economic organisation       338.094
France : Economic planning            338.944

The enquirer may with justification wonder why these three topics are not all together at a single location.

For the rest, the solid advantage of economy and systematic working gained at the cost of a disproportionately small loss to user convenience remain as outlined in Chapter IX.

### BRITISH CATALOGUE OF MUSIC SUBJECT INDEXING

In addition to its use in the *British National Bibliography*, chain procedure is also employed for the subject index of the *British Catalogue of Music.*[6] This publication is classified by a scheme with a fully faceted structure and synthesising notation.

This notation does not reflect the hierarchy of terms (except fortuitously) so that subject index entries cannot be derived from mere inspection of the class symbols, but require consideration of the schedules. The notation is, however, virtually co-extensive with the descriptions of the material recorded, so that no equivalent to the [1] device, as used in *B.N.B.*, is needed.

The problem of unsought terms is much less acute for an index to a special subject field than for one covering the whole of knowledge. Almost every term produced by chain procedure from the *B.C.M.* classification is likely to be looked for by enquirers, and the unsought residue are practically self-evident.

The main departure from earlier chain procedural technique is that prepositions are regularly used to link pairs of qualifier terms where the sense so requires. Thus the entry

>     Organ : Arrangements : Recorder      VSK/R

is ambiguous except for someone who has learned how to unravel the composite classification symbol. The nature of the relationship between Organ, Recorder, and Arrangements is made clear by the insertion of a single preposition

>     Organ : Arrangements for recorder      VSK/R

Once the relationship between Arrangements and Recorder has thus been made clear, that between Organ and Arrangements can safely be left to inference, namely that the works referred to are arrangements *from* organ works.

Some general steps have also been taken to modify the chain order of qualifiers. The order of components in class symbols is as follows :

>     Instrument performing
>             Number of instruments or parts
>                     Accompanying instrument
>                             Number of accompanying instruments or parts
>                                     Arrangement from . . .
>                                             Form
>                                                     Character

Chain procedure, reversing this would give

>     Character : Form : Arrangement from . . . : Number of accompanying
>             instruments : Accompanying instruments : Number of instru-
>             ments or parts for performance : Instrument performing

There are two substantial objections to this order. It cites the names of accompanying instruments before those of the main. instrument (or voice) for which performance is intended. Secondly it gives the word denoting size of combination or number of instruments/voices or parts before the names of the instruments/voices concerned. A modified order designed to eliminate these features has therefore been adopted. It may be illustrated concretely by

> Film music : Dances : String octet : Arrangements for string orchestra :
> Accompanied by piano solo    RXMPQK/RXNNH/JR

This may be compared with the same subject with the qualifiers arranged in strict chain order

> Film music : Dances : Octets : String instruments : Arrangements for
> piano solo : Accompanying orchestra : String instruments

Many of the entities connected with musical performance are designated only by aggregations of the names of the constituent instruments. At first it seemed that it might be possible to index these upon the lines of orthodox chain procedure avoiding permutation. For instance SQPLSR – Works for viola and cello could be indexed

| | |
|---|---|
| Viola | SQ |
| Cello & viola | SQPLSR |

Difficulties begin, however, when we have arrangements from works originally for viola and cello. If arranged, for instance, for clarinet and bassoon, they take the symbol VVPLVWK/SQPLSR. By analogy with the previous example, this is indexed as

> Viola : Arrangements for clarinet & bassoon    VVPLVWK/SQ
> Cello & viola : Arrangements for clarinet & bassoon
>                      VVPLVWK/SQPLSR

The first of these entries will not do. It conveys the unmistakable sense that the work was originally for solo viola. The difficulty seems capable of solution upon one of two lines. Either we can use some such clumsy construction as

> Viola (solo or ensemble, including combinations with a second instru-
> ment) : Arrangements for clarinet & bassoon
>                    VVPLVWK/SQ

or we can permute, giving

> Viola & cello : Arrangements for clarinet & bassoon
>                    VVPLVWK/SQPLSR

However, this means that we must also permute the entry for the simple viola and cello duet, since we cannot use 'Viola & cello' for the arrangements, whilst depending on the generic entry 'Viola' for the unarranged works. No satisfactory answer has so far been devised to meet this problem.

For combinations of three instruments or instrumental groups, the structure of the classification and chain procedure permit certain economies in permutation. As an example we may give NUV – A work for clarinet, strings, and keyboard ensemble. This is indexed as follows :

| | |
|---|---|
| Clarinet, strings & keyboard : Chamber music | NUV |
| Woodwind, strings & keyboard : Chamber music | NUP |
| Wind, strings & keyboard : Chamber music | NU |
| Keyboard, wind & strings : Chamber music | NU |
| Strings, keyboard & wind : Chamber music | NU |

It will be noticed that permutation is carried out at the generic level only, and not fully there. Each of the terms is brought in turn to the entry word position, without disturbing the order of the other two.

In this account of the application of chain procedure to the *British Catalogue of Music*, a relatively large amount of space has been given to the modifications found necessary and the residual problems. It should be realised, however, that the vast majority of problems in the subject indexing of music have found easy solutions. As the material in the catalogue accumulates, it will become the only large-scale application of chain procedure, uncomplicated by the structural irregularities of a traditional classification scheme.

## NOTES AND REFERENCES

[1] The Decimal Classification as used in this chapter and later means the 14th edition occasionally helped out by the 15th edition.

[2] See Mills, J. *Chain indexing and the classified catalogue*, Libr. Assoc. Record, Vol. 57, 1955, pp. 141–148.

[3] But see Chapter IX (p. 109) in which this same entry word is used to show that an apparently unsought term may be sought by enquirers who understand themselves to be consulting a catalogue limited to a particular subject or field of interest.

[4] I am indebted to D. J. Foskett for this information.

[5] Metcalfe, J. *Information indexing and subject cataloguing* (New York, 1957), pp. 159–166.

[6] *British Catalogue of Music*, 1957–. In progress.

# CHAPTER XI

# CHAIN PROCEDURE AND THE ALPHABETICO-SPECIFIC CATALOGUE

WE are now in a position to resume the discussion of the alphabetico-specific catalogue from the point at which we left it at the end of Chapter VII. The conclusion had been reached that this form of catalogue posed two main problems. The first was the order of components in compound subjects. To this problem Chapter VI attempted a partial answer based upon the relative significance of components in a compound and the manner in which they were related in the composite concept. The second problem was how to systematise the signalling of subject relationships by connective references. This was treated in a general way by the suggestion that the system of connective references needed to be based upon a fully worked out scheme of subject relationships such as is found in a classification scheme. In the last three chapters we have been making what is really an oblique approach to this latter problem. We have examined verbal indexes to classified catalogues and, in particular, one method of constructing them which is related in a most intimate way to the structure of the classification scheme in use. It will have occurred to many readers to ask whether chain procedural methods applied to the alphabetico-specific catalogue would not at the same time provide that classificatory basis for the scheme of connective references which has been declared so desirable.

A general affirmative answer can be given immediately, with the proviso that we should not expect chain procedural answers to problems of component order to be directly useful to the alphabetico-specific catalogue. In the classified catalogue, chain procedural component order in the index complements the manner in which the same components are formed into a composite subject concept in the classified file. Where there is no classified file, we should expect different, though perhaps not entirely different, principles of component order to apply. An attempt to sketch some of the background of these principles is made in Chapter VI. If we can combine the conclusions reached there with the chain procedural method, we shall have

attained a practical solution to both of the problems – component
order and systematisation of references.

For the subject index to the classified catalogue, chain procedural
analysis yields a specific entry together with a series of generic entries.
Similarly for the alphabetico-specific catalogue it yields the verbal raw
material (though as we shall see, not always in the finished form) of the
specific subject heading and of the series of hierarchical 'see also'
references which lead back to the subject heading.

Thus, to revert to examples cited in connection with subject indexing
for the classified catalogue in the last chapter, the D.C. symbol 331.283
produces the following list of terms :

    3    Agriculture
    8    Special industries
    2    Wages
    1    Labour
    3    Economics
    3    Social sciences

As before, we reject the False Link which constitutes the second of the
terms in the above list, and, supplying the necessary qualifiers, which
in the context of the alphabetico-specific catalogue, we shall hence-
forth call subheadings, we are left with

    ARICULTURE, Wages, Economics
    WAGES, Economics
    LABOUR, Economics
    ECONOMICS
    SOCIAL SCIENCES

The first item in this list is the specific subject heading for a book on
Agricultural wages, classified at 331.283. The subsequent items
represent the hierarchical references, each of which is linked to the one
above it. The final form of this subject heading material is therefore

    AGRICULTURE, Wages, Economics          (Subject heading)
    WAGES, Economics   *see also* AGRICULTURE, Wages, Economics
    LABOUR, Economics   *see also* WAGES, Economics
    ECONOMICS   *see also* LABOUR, Economics
    SOCIAL SCIENCES   *see also* ECONOMICS

As in the case of the classified catalogue subject index, the chain procedure from D.C. symbols must be based upon the real rather than the
notational hierarchy; and some means, such as the *B.N.B.* verbal extension after [1], must be employed to specify topics for which the

Decimal Classification gives no specific notation. Thus for the D.C. symbol 251, we have

PREACHING                                 (Subject Heading)
PASTORAL WORK, Christianity   *see also* PREACHING
CHURCH   *see also* PASTORAL WORK, Christianity
CHRISTIANITY   *see also* CHURCH
RELIGION   *see also* CHRISTIANITY

As an example of a topic without precise specification in the D.C., we may take Ferroelectricity, given in *B.N.B.* as 537.2 [1] – Dielectrics. Ferroelectricity.

FERROELECTRICITY                          (Subject Heading)
DIELECTRICS, Physics   *see also* FERROELECTRICITY
ELECTROSTATICS, Physics   *see also* DIELECTRICS, Physics
ELECTRICITY, Physics   *see also* ELECTROSTATICS, Physics
PHYSICS   *see also* ELECTRICITY, Physics
SCIENCE   *see also* PHYSICS

### MODIFIED CHAIN PROCEDURE

These are all extremely simple cases in which the first term produced by chain procedure is the entry word of the subject heading, and the order of the terms which follow represents the order of the syndetic references. Some cases in which modification is required are now introduced. The D.C. symbol 338.921763 – Economic Planning of the Sheep Farming Industry, is analysed by chain procedure as follows :

3   Sheep
6   Livestock
7   Special
1   Agriculture
2   Special
9   Planning
8   Organisation
3   Economics
3   Social sciences

Eliminating the two False Links indicated by the word 'Special' and treating 'Organisation' as an unsought term, we produce from this basic analysis the following qualified list :

Sheep, Agriculture, Planning, Economics
Livestock, Agriculture, Planning, Economics
Agriculture, Planning, Economics
Planning, Economics

Economics
Social sciences

When we envisage the above as subject headings in an alphabetical
subject catalogue, we notice that the fourth item 'Planning, Economics'
contravenes the principle laid down in Chapter VI for component
order. 'Planning' has a wider connotation and is more abstract than
'Economics'. In amplified phrase the compound means 'Planning of
economic affairs' and is an example of Type 1 in the Relationship
Table. Component order as given by chain procedure has therefore to
be reversed. The alphabetical catalogue chain is thus

SHEEP, Agriculture, Economic planning        (Subject Heading)
LIVESTOCK, Agriculture, Economic planning   see also SHEEP,
    Agriculture, Economic planning
AGRICULTURE, Economic planning  see also LIVESTOCK, Economic
    planning
ECONOMICS, Planning  see also  AGRICULTURE, Economic
    planning
SOCIAL SCIENCES  see also ECONOMICS

In accordance with the modification already suggested, 'Planning' has
now disappeared as an entry word, and the two hierarchical stages
represented in the basic analysis by 'Economics' and 'Planning' have
become elided. But we must still make provision for access to the
subject from the word 'Planning', and to this end we make the following inversion reference

PLANNING, Economics  see  ECONOMICS, Planning

We may generalise this situation by the following rule : Where
component order, either at specific or generic level, as given by chain
procedure, conflicts with the Significance formula (see Chapter VI) or
the Relationship Table, chain procedure order is to be amended
accordingly, but the compound in chain procedure order is always to
be given inversion reference to the compound in modified order.

It will be noticed that the concept 'Planning, Economics' above has
similarly undergone transposition of components in being rendered
as a phrase in the subheadings.

One possible result of the need to modify chain procedure component order is that the leading word of the first item in the qualified
list is not necessarily the entry word of the subject heading. Thus, in the
example 616.12075 Diagnosis of Heart Diseases, we have the qualified
list

Diagnosis, Heart, Diseases
Heart, Diseases
Circulatory system, Diseases
Diseases, Medicine
Medicine

The first item as an amplified phrase is 'Diagnosis of diseases of the heart' – an Action upon an Action already affecting a Thing. This is a combination of Types 3 and 1 in the Relationship Table. This is incompatible with the chain procedure order given above. The alphabetico-specific catalogue chain is therefore given as

HEART, Diseases, Diagnosis          (Subject Heading)
CIRCULATORY SYSTEM, Diseases  *see also* HEART, Diseases
DISEASES, Medicine  *see also* CIRCULATORY SYSTEM, Diseases
MEDICINE  *see also* DISEASES, Medicine

As before, an inversion reference must be supplied for the suppressed term. We therefore add

DIAGNOSIS, Heart, Diseases  *see* HEART, Diseases, Diagnosis

In the example dealing with Sheep Farming it was said that the modification of chain procedure order 'Planning, Economics' resulted in the elision of the two hierarchical stages given in the basic analysis. This elision is not always complete. If, for instance, we had previously decided to treat 'Organisation' not as unsought, but merely as calling for suppression from the entry word position in the chain, we should have ended with

ECONOMICS, Planning *see also* AGRICULTURE, Economic planning
ECONOMICS, Organisation  *see also* ECONOMICS, Planning
SOCIAL SCIENCES  *see also* ECONOMICS

It will be noticed that we have a *see also* reference from one subheading to another under the same entry word. The same phenomenon (which can occur only when the chain procedural component order is modified) is illustrated in the following example:

Extraction of the venom of snakes, classified at 598.12[1] – SECRETIONS. VENOM. EXTRACTION

The basic analysis is

[1] Extraction
[1] Venom
[1] Secretions
2 Snakes

1 Reptiles
8 Birds & reptiles   (False Link)
596 Vertebrates
9 Zoology
574 Biology
5 Science

The qualified list is

> Extraction, Venom, Snakes
> Venom, Snakes, Zoology
> Secretions, Snakes
> Snakes
> Reptiles
> Vertebrates
> Zoology
> Biology
> Science

The chain procedural order in the compounds here is not in accordance with alphabetical specific catalogue requirements. The first item is a combination of Types 2 and 4 in the Relationship Table. Extraction of Venom is an Action upon a Material, and Venom of Snakes is a Material belonging to a Thing. These two ideas are represented in subject heading form as 'VENOM, Extraction' and 'SNAKES, Venom' respectively. The combined subject heading is therefore

> SNAKES, Venom, Extraction

The chain of references is

> VERTEBRATES   *see also* SNAKES
> ZOOLOGY   *see also* VERTEBRATES
> BIOLOGY   *see also* ZOOLOGY
> SCIENCE   *see also* BIOLOGY

Assuming 'Extraction' to be an unsought term, the following *see* references are needed :

> VENOM, Snakes   *see* SNAKES, Venom
> SECRETIONS, Snakes   *see* SNAKES, Venom

The first of these is an inversion reference of the ordinary type necessitated by modification of the chain procedural component order. The second would be required only if there were no material in the collection upon Secretions of Snakes specifically. The link represented in the qualified list by 'Secretions, Snakes' would normally appear in the alphabetical subject catalogue as

> SNAKES, Secretions

being another example of Type 4 in the Relationship Table. In the present instance this would lead to the reference

SNAKES, Secretions   *see also* SNAKES, Venom

Such a reference would, without doubt, be useful, but it seems legitimate to expect the enquirer to search all subheadings under a particular heading unless their number is very great. This reference is therefore omitted. However, we have to provide access from 'Secretions', and this is done by means of a *see* reference to 'Snakes, Venom' as shown above. Any synonyms of 'Secretions, Snakes' would need similar treatment.

The situation would have been more complicated but for the fact that 'Snakes' in the qualified list above was a term without a subheading. We may examine a less simple example, namely, Fatigue of Metals in Engineering, classified at 620.18 [1] – FATIGUE.

The basic analysis is

| | |
|---|---|
| [1] | Fatigue |
| 8 | Metals |
| *620.11/9* | Materials, Strength of |
| 1 | Applied mechanics & Strength of Materials   (False Link) |
| 0 | General Works   (False Link) |
| 2 | Engineering |
| 6 | Technology |

The qualified list is

> Fatigue, Metals, Engineering
> Metals, Engineering
> Materials, Strength of, Engineering
> Engineering
> Technology

The alphabetico-specific catalogue chain is

> METALS, Fatigue, Engineering                (Subject Heading)
> [METALS, Engineering  *see also* METALS, Fatigue, Engineering]
> MATERIALS, Strength, Engineering  *see also* METALS, Fatigue, Engineering
> ENGINEERING  *see also* MATERIALS, Strength, Engineering
> TECHNOLOGY  *see also* ENGINEERING

Inversion references are required as follows :

> FATIGUE, Metals  *see* METALS, Fatigue
> STRENGTH, Materials  *see* MATERIALS, Strength

The subject 'Engineering aspects of the Fatigue of Metals' is a combination of Types 6 and 7 in the Relationship Table. Fatigue of Metals is a case of Property of Material, and Engineering is a viewpoint. The

bracketed reference above from 'METALS, Engineering' is the next
logical link in the chain, but as it directs to another subheading under
METALS, it is omitted. The succeeding reference from 'MATERIALS,
Engineering' bypasses this omitted stage, referring directly to
'METALS, Fatigue, Engineering'. The use of such a bypassing refer-
ence does not preclude the use of the normal syndetic reference

> MATERIALS, Strength, Engineering    *see also* METALS,
> Engineering

whenever there are documents specifically on the latter subject.

Modifications of chain procedural component order will therefore
call for some or all of the following modifications of normal syndetic
referencing :

(a) Inversion references are made from all suppressed terms

(b) If the term transposed to entry word position appears in the
qualified list without subheading, the link in the chain corresponding
to the unqualified word will become redundant

(c) If the term transposed to entry word position appears also in the
qualified list as subheading, then the stage in hierarchical referencing
corresponding to the latter is omitted. It is bypassed by a reference
connecting the headings above and below it in the hierarchy.

In the examples so far given, recourse has from time to time been
had to the Relationship Table to ascertain component order, and
where this has been found to vary from chain procedure order, the
former prevails with the consequent adjustments to the referencing
already described. Similar adjustments are made when chain procedure
order is in conflict with the conventional treatment of Subject –
Locality compounds. The example which follows will make this clear :

> Lead mining in Lancashire, classed at 622.344094272

The basic analysis is:

| | |
|---|---|
| 2 | Lancashire |
| 7 | North Western England & Yorkshire   (False Link) |
| 2 | Great Britain |
| 4 | Europe |
| 9 | History |
| 0 | (Connective device.   False Link) |
| 4 | Lead |
| 4 | Metals |
| 3 | Special Materials   (False Link) |
| 2 | Mining |
| 2 | Engineering |
|   | Technology |

Treating 'Great Britain', 'Europe', and 'History' as unsought terms in this context, we have the qualified list

> Lancashire, Lead, Mining
> Lead, Mining
> Metals, Mining
> Mining
> Engineering
> Technology

From this the alphabetico-specific catalogue chain is derived as follows :

> LEAD, Mining – Lancashire                    (Subject Heading)
> METALS, Mining   *see also* LEAD, Mining
> MINING   *see also* METALS, Mining
> ENGINEERING   *see also* MINING
> TECHNOLOGY   *see also* ENGINEERING

Because 'Lancashire' has been suppressed from entry word position, an inversion reference is needed

> LANCASHIRE, Lead mining   *see*  LEAD, Mining – Lancashire

Class numbers terminating in Form Divisions are treated in exactly the same fashion as the preceding example. The term designating the form or common subject appears at the beginning of the qualified list, but is relegated to a subheading in the alphabetico-specific catalogue chain. Form terms rarely need an inversion reference in a general library.

A periodical on Commercial Potato Growing, classified at 633.49105 is analysed basically as

| | |
|---|---|
| 5 | Periodicals |
| o | (Connective Device.   False Link) |
| 1 | Potatoes |
| 9 | Tubers |
| 4 | (An extraneous term not belonging to this hierarchy) |
| 3 | Crops |
| 3 | Agriculture |
| 6 | Technology |

From this the following qualified list is derived :

> Periodicals, Potatoes, Agriculture
> Potatoes, Agriculture
> Tubers, Agriculture
> Crops, Agriculture
> Agriculture
> Technology

The alphabetico-specific catalogue chain is

> POTATOES, Agriculture – periodicals
> TUBERS, Agriculture   *see also* POTATOES, Agriculture
> CROPS, Agriculture   *see also* TUBERS, Agriculture
> TECHNOLOGY   *see also* AGRICULTURE

In all of the above examples subheadings have been preferred to phrases, and some reasons for this general preference have been given in Chapter III. However, there are occasions when phrases must be used. Their employment, either out of necessity or because they are preferred to subheadings, involves only slight modifications of the technique outlined in this chapter. There are sound reasons for making references from inverted forms of phrases, and these will usually make redundant one of the generic links indicated in the qualified list. Thus, if we have

> ORGANIC CHEMISTRY                    (Subject Heading)
> CHEMISTRY, Organic   *see* ORGANIC CHEMISTRY
> (Inversion reference)

we do not need the hierarchical reference

> CHEMISTRY   *see also* ORGANIC CHEMISTRY

The reference

> SCIENCE   *see also* CHEMISTRY

is, of course, still valid.

### MULTI-ASPECT SUBJECTS

When everything has been said for classification as a necessary foundation for the system of relationship references in the alphabetical catalogue, there remains the objection voiced by Miss Pettee, to which allusion was made earlier. Classification separates concrete unities according to the various aspects represented by main class headings. Only the alphabetical subject catalogue can offer a heading for a subject in its full integrity. If the alphabetical subject headings are to be derived from class symbols in the manner suggested, will this valuable property not be lost? We must admit the general validity of this point of view in so far as it relates to classification schemes currently used. There is, on the other hand, no *a priori* reason why classification schemes should not accommodate subjects in their most general aspects. It is just that schemes have not so far been constructed to achieve this. They have been designed to fit a literature that has consisted for the most part of documents treating of a limited number of aspects of a subject. However, the changing pattern of knowledge is itself beginning to take account of subjects as unities. Recently we have seen the beginning of a literature on such generalities as Organisation, Management (not merely Business Management), and Communication. Future classifications will have to be designed to accommodate unitary concepts of this sort. This issue should not be confused with that of a 'one place classification' which is clearly an impossibility. No classification can be devised which will assemble all documents appertaining to a given subject at a single location. The ability to provide a general place for any subject is quite another matter and quite within the realm of possibility.

The objection must, however, be faced within the context of present schemes of classification. When a book, let us say, on Railways treated generally is classified by the D.C., two policies are possible. We may either decide that a particular symbol, for example 385, shall be the location for Railways in general as well as for Railway Economics, or we can provide added entries at such numbers as 625 and 656 to cover the less prominently treated aspects. In the first case, there is an element of subterfuge, by which the subject cataloguer should not be deceived when he comes to translate the class symbol into verbal data for subject headings. If the second policy is used, the need for added entries will be a sufficient signal to the subject cataloguer that he has here a general book on Railways, not confined to the economic aspects. In either case the subject heading will be

RAILWAYS   (not RAILWAYS, Economics).

The two subsidiary classified entries are given no counterpart in the alphabetico-specific catalogue. Neither need any attempt be made to provide references to the general heading RAILWAYS from related subjects. It is unlikely that the same heading amplified by subheadings will not have occurred already in the catalogue. The references to and from such amplified headings already determined by chain procedure will provide sufficient connection between the general subject and others related to it.

## THE RESULTANT ALPHABETICAL SUBJECT CATALOGUE

We may now make an attempt to draw some general conclusions on the exploitation of classification on behalf of the alphabetico-specific catalogue. In the first place, chain procedural analysis of the position of a subject within a classification scheme can provide the verbal raw material for the subject heading and for the chain of references leading down to it. In order to extract this material competently, the subject cataloguer must refer directly to the real hierarchical structure of the classification schedule, and not merely to the ingredients of the notation : he must also be able to elaborate the published schedule in order to specify subjects not provided for by the classification maker, but he need not elaborate the notation. The result is a properly articulated network of references signalling hierarchical relationship between subjects. Because of errors of judgment and gross mistakes in the classification scheme, the system of references may not be ideal in every particular – but since it is a system, it is to be preferred to the multidimensional maze described in Chapter VII. It will result in fewer hierarchical references, in many cases, than are prescribed in the Library of Congress *Subject Headings*, and therefore some searches in the catalogue may demand from the enquirer a greater number of shifts from one part of the catalogue to the other than would be needed if the Library of Congress list, rather than a classification scheme, were used as a basis for the subject headings. On the other hand, a plethora of references to related subjects, to all appearances unsystematically chosen, hardly encourages systematic searching. Finally, with a relative paucity of downward-directing references, the insertion of a corresponding set of upward-directing references becomes feasible. As has been mentioned in Chapter III, upward-directing references are essential if the alphabetical subject catalogue is to emulate the facilities for search offered by the classified catalogue. Once the chain of downward-directing references has been obtained, it is, of course, purely a mechanical matter to produce a corresponding set, pointing, as it were, in the opposite direction. The upward-directing references have been omitted in the illustrations given in this chapter in order not to encumber the explanation of subject heading derivation from classification data. It is essential that they should be added.

Chain procedural analysis provides, as we have seen, an indication of the content of the subject heading and hierarchical references, but not necessarily of their form. The considerations for deciding component order were detailed in Chapter VI, and they do not always coincide in their results with the order given by chain procedure. Where, in the light of the Relationship Table, chain procedure order needs modification, supplementary inversion references may be required to provide access to a term otherwise not chosen as entry word. Furthermore, some hierarchical stages may become redundant, and steps may be required to avoid the emergence of references directing from one subheading to another under the same entry word. The adjustment of these situations is a relatively simple matter.

The argument of this Chapter has been very largely against the background of the Decimal Classification. The development of chain procedure has, however, been closely associated with the Colon Classification, and it is legitimate to enquire whether chain procedural analysis of symbols drawn from that scheme might not offer self-sufficient answers to problems of component order. Facets in classification represent relations between subjects, therefore we might expect a fully faceted classification to provide full solutions to questions of component order, which would be in agreement with the Relationship Table. Ranganathan has used chain procedure in this way in his *Dictionary Catalogue Code* but is now ready to admit that the results are not entirely satisfactory and that the whole question needs further investigation. It seems likely that the ultimate appeal will still have to lie in the relationships between components. It is within the bounds of possibility that most of the relationships concerned could be built into or made explicit in future developments of the Colon Classification, but until this is done, the only practical approach to the difficulties seems to be along the lines of Chapter VI and reliance upon the meagre hints offered by the way in which subject relationship is expressed in natural language.

This chapter has so far limited its concern to the hierarchical references in an alphabetico-specific subject catalogue. The collateral references between subjects may also be based upon a classification scheme. The control exercised by the latter is looser than for the hierarchical references, and largely negative in that it merely ensures that two terms so connected are co-ordinate members at the same hierarchical level and in the same facet. Collateral references produced under these conditions cannot be used to make good the inadequacies of non-specific subject entry. The classification scheme does not at any point imply a positive direction that a collateral reference is required. Not all subjects which stand side-by-side in the classification scheme are related in a way which is significant for searching : non-significant collocation in the classification scheme should not be reproduced in the guise of collateral references in the alphabetico-specific catalogue. Pairs of subjects which utilise a common or parallel set of principles or overlap in a shared area of knowledge will normally need to be connected by collateral references, but where the relationship is less close, only the cataloguer's knowledge of the subjects themselves can determine whether a reference is necessary. It may be pointed out that collateral references are not absolutely vital in an alphabetico-specific catalogue equipped with upward-directing hierarchical references. If the latter references are present, it follows that any subject is linked to its collateral by way of the generic term common to both. Thus an enquirer at 'RADIO, Engineering' is reminded of the presence of material on Television engineering by means of the following pair of hierarchical references, the first being upward-directing, and the second downward.

> RADIO, Engineering. *For related topics see* COMMUNICATION, Engineering
>
> COMMUNICATIONS, Engineering *see also* TELEVISION, Engineering

# Chapter XII

## GROUP ARRANGEMENT IN THE SUBJECT INDEX

THE hesitant use of specific subject entry, as well as the less explicable phrase inversions in Library of Congress practice, are to be attributed to a wish to avoid the physical separation of entries on related topics. Ranganathan[1] has seized upon this phenomenon in dictionary catalogue practice as evidence of the inherent superiority of the classified catalogue. We need not accept this contention, but we are obliged to recognise that, although the deliberate assemblage of related subjects is incompatible with the alphabetico-specific principle, it probably corresponds with a very deep-seated expectation on the part of the user.

This expectation has also run counter to some of the results of chain procedural subject indexing for the classified catalogue. Metcalfe appears to be unfavourably impressed with the sequence of qualifiers which he found in the B.N.B. subject index under the heading 'Photography'.[2] The same logical disorder will apply to any purely alphabetical sequence of subject terms. The chain procedural subject index requires the reader to find first the leading word of the sought compound subject, and then to peruse a sub-sequence of qualifier terms under the leading word. The verb 'peruse' is used advisedly here. By and large, the terms used as qualifier subheadings are relatively insignificant. Enquirers often have in mind only one significant word, the entry word. About the remaining terms needed to define the desired subject, they are frequently vague; not consciously seeking a definite term, but hoping to find one in the list of subheadings which will cover the topic being sought. Hence, after the entry word has been found, searching becomes a matter of reading through all the subheadings in the index rather than attempting to find some definite secondary term.

The question therefore arises whether it would not be better to group qualifiers in the classified catalogue subject index into a few subject categories, in order to save the enquirer the labour of scanning the full alphabetical series. It may be argued that if the number of categories is not too large, their constant repetition in the index would make them familiar and easy for the enquirer. There is also likely to be a subsidiary advantage in grouping qualifiers. Ambiguities of meaning arising out of the lack of relationship indicators in chain index entries, are likely to disappear if all qualifiers in a particular relationship with the entry word form a compact block. For instance

Photography : Periodicals

in the context

Photography : Advertising
Photography : Periodicals
Photography : Surgical pathology
Photography : Visual aids : Teaching

would appear to mean 'Photography in periodicals'. In another context

Photography : Bibliography
Photography : Exhibitions
Photography : Periodicals
Photography : Special libraries
Photography : Theses

its meaning would probably be guessed as 'Periodicals on photography'. As in natural language, context may be exploited to make meanings clear.

### SUBHEADING ARRANGEMENT BY MAIN CLASSES

One obvious and mechanical procedure for grouping the qualifier terms is to form groups on the basis of the Main Classes or Divisions of the classification scheme, using the class symbol attached to each entry as a guide. Let us consider the following set of entries :

| | |
|---|---|
| Labour : Business management : Business education | 378.996583 |
| Labour : Department stores : Business | 658.871[1] |
| Labour : Ethics : Personal Christianity | 241.[1] |
| Labour : Food requirements : Medicine | 612.3951 |
| Labour : Obstetrics | 618.4 |
| Labour : Office organisation | 651.34 |
| Labour : Shipping operations | 656.[1] |
| Labour : Sociology : Christianity | 261.[1] |

This is straight alphabetical sub-arrangement as used in *B.N.B.* If we re-arrange in Decimal Classification order, having first extracted the homonym 'Labour : Obstetrics', we have

| | |
|---|---|
| Labour : Ethics : Personal Christianity | 241.[1] |
| Labour : Sociology : Christianity | 261.[1] |
| Labour : Business management : Business education | 378.996583 |
| Labour : Food requirements : Physiology : Medicine | 612.3951 |
| Labour : Office management | 651.34 |
| Labour : Shipping : Transport operations | 656.[1] |
| Labour : Department stores : Business | 658.871[1] |
| | |
| Labour : Obstetrics | 618.4 |

We have now some grouping, but the arrangement is scarcely more satisfactory or readily understood than the purely alphabetical one. We may, however, try the effect of retaining the above order, but with transposition of qualifiers, so that the grouping term immediately follows the entry word

| | |
|---|---|
| Labour : Christianity : Personal ethics | 241.[1] |
| Labour : Christianity : Sociology | 261.[1] |
| Labour : Business education : Business management | 378.996583 |
| Labour : Medicine : Physiology : Food requirements | 612.3951 |
| Labour : Business methods : Office organisation | 651.34 |
| Labour : Business methods : Shipping | 656.[1] |
| Labour : Business methods : Department stores | 658.871[1] |
| | |
| Labour : Obstetrics | 618.4 |

This is a distinct advance, though the ordering of the groups formed still appears capable of improvement, and the fourth entry seems to have suffered badly from the transposition. To give some idea of the effect of idiosyncracies of particular classification schemes, some of the same subjects are given below as indexed if classified by the Colon scheme. Owing to the fact that facet order for the first and fifth items above is not the same in the Colon Scheme as in the Decimal Classification, it is only possible to give their containing genera as subjects which will be indexed with the entry word 'Labour'

| | |
|---|---|
| Labour : Medicine, Industrial | L9X : 95 |
| Labour : Ethics, Personal | R417(X : 95) |
| Labour : Ethics : Christianity | R(Q6)4(X : 95) |
| Labour : Education : Economics : Management | T : 2(X : 8–95) |
| Labour : Economics : Shipping | X425 : 95 |
| Labour : Economics : Department stores | X528 : 95 |
| | |
| Labour : Obstetrics | L9F : 35 |

### FUNDAMENTAL CLASS SUBHEADINGS

This grouping does not appear to be significantly better than that obtained using the Decimal Classification. The notational component X : 95 which occurs in all the composite Colon Classification symbols above does, however, emphasise a fact that has so far been overlooked; namely, that the concept Labour belongs fundamentally to that of Economics, irrespective of the special context in which it may occur. The fact that the subheading 'Economics' appears in only a proportion of the entries tends to obscure this. Labour and Economics can never be dissociated, but it is nevertheless possible to have aspects of both Labour and Economics which transcend the field of Economics proper. If we reconsider the topics given in the last illustration, we shall see that the aspects of Labour given there comprise three groups; (a) purely economic aspects, the compound class symbols for which *commence* with the digit X; (b) aspects which though in themselves not of directly economic character, none the less denote activities which support economic motives; (c) transcendental aspects which consider the subject from a viewpoint external to economics. On this basis, the subjects may be re-grouped as follows :

Group (a) aspects – purely economic
> Labour : Shipping : Economics     X425 : 95
> Labour : Departmental stores : Economics     X528 : 95
> Labour : Office management     X : 8M : 95

Group (b) aspects – supporting economic activity
> Labour : Management : Business education     T : 2(X : 8–95)
> Labour : Industrial medicine     L9X : 95

Group (c) aspects – transcendental
> Labour : Personal ethics     R417(X : 95)
> Labour : Ethics : Christian philosophy     R(Q6)4(X : 95)

This would seem to be a more helpful sequence than that obtained by following classification order. A further example is now considered from another field :

> Sea : Birds     K96–99555
> Sea : Archæology     V : 7(U25)
> Sea : Fisheries     λ3325 : 7
> Sea : Geography     U25
> Sea : Law     Z,215
> Sea : Warfare     MV45

The recurring notational component 5 does not in itself assist in assigning Sea to its Fundamental Class. However, we can discover the Fundamental Class by asking ourselves what is the context which we use when we try to define 'Sea'? Any definition must begin in geographical terms : 'That part of the earth's surface which . . .', and as the sea is thus uniquely definable in geographical terms, Geography is to be regarded as the Fundamental Class, and the first subheading. In Geography the sea is studied in its broadest aspects. More limited aspects of the study of the sea are represented by the subheadings 'Birds' and 'Archæology'. The remaining subheadings all relate to the use of the sea. 'Fisheries' and 'Warfare' are uses purely and simply, while 'Law' is a set of problems and solutions arising out of the use of the sea. The recommended arrangement would therefore be as follows:

| | | |
|---|---|---|
| Fundamental aspect | | |
| | Sea : Geography | U25 |
| Study aspects | | |
| | Sea : Archæology | V : 7(U25) |
| | Sea : Birds | K96–99555 |
| Use aspects | | |
| | Sea : Fisheries | λ3325 : 7 |
| | Sea : Warfare | MV45 |
| Use aspects – contingent problems | | |
| | Sea : Law | Z,215 |

The first step in organising a helpful arrangement of subject index entry subheadings is to consider which of the qualifier words represents the Fundamental Class to which the entry word concept necessarily always belongs. It has been noted that Labour (apart from its special obstetrical sense) is always an economic phenomenon, even though it may be considered from points of view which are extraneous to economics. Similarly Sea is always a geographical entity. Economics and Geography are the respective Fundamental Classes in these cases. The subheading representing the Fundamental Class precedes all others in arrangement. The remaining subheadings are filed behind it in order of increasing remoteness from the Fundamental Class concept. Subheadings most closely allied to the Fundamental Class follow it immediately, whilst those least related to it are placed in sequence farthest from it. It must be conceded that 'increasing remoteness' and 'most closely allied' are equivocal phrases, yet their import is fairly clear in the examples given. In both cases the main line of division is between economic and utilitarian aspects on the one hand, and non-utilitarian study aspects on the other. In the case of Labour, those aspects which have to do with utilisation come first because the Fundamental Class is Economics. In the second case those aspects which are studies not directly linked with utilisation take precedence, because they include the Fundamental Class Geography.

The following table attempts to amplify the suggestions which have emerged from the examples so far considered :

| Fundamental Class expressed as 1st subheading, or implied where entry word is unqualified | Economics | Useful Arts and Artefacts | Sociology | Science |
|---|---|---|---|---|
| Remaining aspects in order of arrangement | Field of application | Field of application | Social role | Other scientific aspects |
| | Special economic aspects | Technical aspects | Social activity | Fields of use |
| | Non-economic aspects which support economic activity | Economic aspects | Transcendental non-social aspects | Technical aspects |
| | Transcendental non-economic aspects | Non-economic aspects which support economic activity | Communications aspects | Economic aspects |
| | Communications aspects | Transcendental non-economic and non-technical aspects | | Social aspects |
| | | Communications aspects | | Communications aspects |

Examples of the application of the Table are now given. No Colon Classification symbols are added, because it is felt that once the principle of the Fundamental Class is understood, its discovery in particular cases will offer no difficulty. However, the Decimal Classification is sometimes singularly uninformative on this issue, and the Colon Classification is often a helpful guide in these cases. One term used in the Table has not been introduced before. This is Communications Aspects, which is employed for Educational, Library, Bibliographical and similar aspects concerned with the handling of information about the subject.

**Racial groups** (the Fundamental Class is Sociology. This term may be given first subheading, or omitted as being implied in the unqualified entry phrase)

(*social roles*)
: Economics, Discrimination
: Economics, Labour, Management
: Economics, Consumer groups, Advertising
: Military life
: Politics

(*social activity*)
: Education
: Welfare

(*transcendental non-social aspects*)
: Physical anthropology
: Psychology

(*communications aspects*)
: Depicted in Belles letters

**Photography** (the Fundamental Class is Useful Arts, despite the Decimal Classification)

(*fields of application*)
: Science, Physics, Nuclear
: Science, Astronomy
: Medicine, Clinical
: Journalism

(*economic aspects*)
: Economics
: Economics, Careers

(*communications aspects*)
: Special libraries

**Clothing** (the Fundamental Class is useful Arts)

(*field of application*)
: Children

(*technical aspects*)
: Manufacture

(*economic aspects*)
: Economics, Industries, Careers
: Economics, Industries, Trade Unions

(*transcendental non-technical, non-economic aspects*)
: Social customs

**Radioactivity** (the fundamental class is Physics)

(*other scientific aspects*)
: Chemistry, Practical, Remote control
: Geophysics
: Biology
: Biology, Genetics

(*fields of application*)
: Military technology, Weapons
: Nuclear power
: Medicine, Diagnosis

(*problems arising from application*)
: Sanitation, Air pollution, Dust

(*communications aspects*)
: Bibliography

**Retailing** (the fundamental class is Economics)

(*fields of application*)
: Clothing
: Domestic gas appliances
: Textiles

(*special economic aspects*)
: Co-operative societies
: Careers

## OTHER PRACTICAL CONSIDERATIONS

Classified groupings of subheadings, combined as shown in these examples with inversion of qualifiers, will probably be preferable to alphabetically arranged indexes to classified catalogues of over 100,000 items. They do, however, admit a considerable additional complexity into the process of preparing the catalogue. The groups cannot be consistently be derived from the classification scheme. In a card catalogue, without benefit of panoramic survey, the leading card for each entry word will need a full synopsis showing the method of arranging the subheadings. Classified catalogues of smaller collections may with advantage employ the grouping principle for subheadings under localities. These are usually the longest lists of subheadings in any chain procedure index, and grouping can be based simply upon the order of the classification, possibly with some adjustment of inconveniently placed classes and divisions. The following compares an alphabetical list of subheadings after place heading taken from the *B.N.B.* with the same topics arranged in D.C. classification order.

Subjects in D.C. class 300 have been taken from their numerical position and placed after those in class 900.

France

: Architecture
: Ballet
: British forces : Memorials : World War 2
: Caves
: Caves : Art : Prehistory
: Concentration camps
: Cookery
: Economic conditions
: Folk tales
: Foreign policy
: Foreign trade
: Hauntings
: History
: Hotels
: Infantry : Military forces
: Local government
: Lodgings for the poor : Social welfare
: Military resources
: Mountaineering
: Murder trials
: Politics
: Postal services
: Precast concrete : Structural engineering
: Railways
: Restaurants
: Royal residences: Architecture
: Rulers : Lives
: Russian foreign policy
: State trials
: Textiles : Industrial design
: Trade unions
: World War 2

: Psychical phenomena, Hauntings
: Geology, Caves
: Prehistory, Art, Caves
: Technology, Engineering, Structural, Precast concrete
: Domestic economy, Cooking
: Domestic economy, Hotels
: Domestic economy, Restaurants
: Architecture
: Architecture, Royal residences
: Industrial design, Textiles
: Entertainment, Ballet
: Sports, Mountaineering
: Biography, Rulers
: History
: History, World War 2
: History, World War 2, British memorials
: Politics
: Politics, Foreign relations
: Politics, Foreign relations, Russia
: Economic conditions
: Economics, Labour, Trade unions
: Law, Criminal, Trials, Murder
: Law, Criminal, Trials, State
: Public administration, Local government
: Military resources
: Military forces, Infantry
: Social welfare, Poor, Lodgings
: Prisons, Concentration camps
: Commerce, Foreign trade
: Commerce, Postal services
: Transport, Railways
: Folklore, Tales

**GROUPED SUBHEADINGS IN THE DICTIONARY CATALOGUE**

It has already been mentioned in Chapter VII that subject subheadings in the Dictionary catalogue of the Library of Congress are not sorted directly into alphabetical order but grouped into separate Form and Locality categories. It may be asked whether the principle of grouped subheadings as here outlined for the subject index to the classified catalogue might not also be applicable to the alphabetical specific catalogue. A difficulty arises here because the alphabetico-specific catalogue, unlike the subject index to the classified catalogue, contains connective references between subject headings. If sub-headings under a given entry word are not arranged alphabetically, then the mere quotation of such compound headings in a reference is no longer a precise direction as to location. It is not possible to refer directly to group subheadings, unless indeed the groups themselves are arranged alphabetically in the manner of the alphabetico-classed catalogue. The examples shown earlier in this chapter suggest that it is by no means easy, and perhaps impossible, to find unequivocal names for the groups with definite catchword value. Expressions such as 'Fields of application' and 'Problems arising from Utilisation' would lead to unbearably ponderous headings if they were inserted immediately after entry words. It is also likely that such helpfulness as the groups may possess would be largely nullified if they were arranged in alpha-betical order. It therefore seems that the practice mentioned on page 78 represents the limits to which the alphabetico-specific catalogue can usefully go in modifying strict alphabetical order of subheadings.

### NOTES AND REFERENCES

[1] Ranganathan, S. R. *Theory of library catalogue* (Madras, 1938), pp. 176–177.
[2] Metcalfe, J. *Information indexing and subject cataloguing* (New York, 1957), p. 164.

# Chapter XIII

# USE AND SEARCH STRATEGY

This chapter will deal with the subject catalogue from the point of view of use. Two extreme types of user will be considered; the uninstructed stranger to catalogues and indexes, and the skilled user. We shall detail some of the forms of assistance needed by the former and give some account of the way in which the skilled user may exploit the catalogue.

## AIDS TO THE ENQUIRER

The uninstructed reader certainly needs instruction — but if offered directly in the form of written 'General Directions for the Use of the Catalogue', its value is questionable. We must expect the enquirer to be too preoccupied with the matter on which he hopes to obtain information to be able to muster any interest in the catalogue for its own sake. If the catalogue is on cards, he must be encouraged by easily comprehensible drawer labels. The information given on these labels is amplified by guide cards within the drawer, the purpose of which is again to encourage and specifically to counteract the forbidding effect of several inches thickness of blank top edge of card. Guide cards break up the catalogue into manageable portions, and they introduce into the card catalogue its sole 'panoramic' feature. They are the chief means by which the enquirer is led to grasp the arrangement and structure of the catalogue. Their effectiveness is circumscribed by certain physical limitations. They must not be placed too close together, otherwise those in front will obscure those behind. This difficulty can be partially overcome by lateral spacing of the guide projections across the width of the drawer, enabling guides to be placed close together but out of lateral alignment. Once the full number of lateral positions has been occupied, a new guide cannot be interpolated unless the subject preceding happens to have a sufficiently large number of entries to allow it to be visible. These physical problems of guiding are especially serious for the systematic section of the classified catalogue. Hierarchy is always associated with indentation on the printed page, and any other use of lateral differentiation of guide position than to indicate subordination is likely to disguise the classified structure of the system. Colour differentiation, often practised, is not a satisfactory substitute for lateral indication of class and species relationship.

Guides in a catalogue are the equivalent of the bold captions which are needed to show the beginnings of the various sections of a printed subject catalogue. Although bold captions do not present the same problems of visibility as the guides in a card catalogue, they are similarly less effective if used at too frequent intervals. Frequency of captions and guides cannot be controlled as a separate factor. We may decide that it is necessary to insert a guide for subject A because there are fifty documents dealing with it. Subjects B and C immediately following have, however, only one entry apiece. If we insert the guide or caption at the beginning of A, we are also obliged to insert two guides very close together at B and C. Only if there is a group name covering B and C can this be avoided. It is clear from this that guiding can never be a mechanical process, but rather a compromise, aiming at ensuring that while subjects represented by a large volume of material are brought into prominence if possible, this does not also necessitate the use of guides for a number of less significant subjects each represented by few entries.

An issue connected with the general approachability of the catalogue which has repeatedly exercised librarians has turned upon the question whether a combined author-title-subject catalogue or index is more easily understood by enquirers than a number of separate catalogues for authors, titles, and subjects respectively. The combined catalogue, it must be said at the outset, has certainly complexities in filing order which the separated catalogue avoids. Some of these are considered in Cutter's Rules 300–314. The same word may stand for a person, subject or place, for a forename or a family name. A title may consist of a single word. Is it to precede or follow subject entries beginning with the same word but including subheadings? The chain procedure form of the names of many corporate bodies will not correspond to the forms prescribed by the Anglo-American Code for author and title entries. Difficulties of this sort can be overcome only by adding complications to the rules for filing, chain procedure, or the Anglo-American Code. In the *B.N.B.* index, for which routine sorting of linotype slugs by the printer is an important factor in keeping down production costs, it has been necessary to assign an ordinal value to punctuation in order to simplify the problems arising from author, title and subject entry filing in the same sequence. Thus a comma, the normal punctuation after an author's family name precedes a colon, the normal punctuation after the entry word in subject index entries. This ensures that a word used both as personal name and as a subject appears first as the personal name and then as subject. The normal punctuation after an author's forename is a full stop. This follows the colon, so that such sequences as

Dickens, Charles : Journalism
Dickens, Charles : Novels : Criticism
Dickens, Charles. Great expectations

are secured automatically.

Separate sequences for authors, titles, and subjects obviate all problems of this nature, but appear to give rise to difficulties and misunderstandings of their own. There seems to be a good deal to be said for unified sequences on general grounds, notwithstanding the complications in arrangement which attend unification. Enquirers are apt to confuse Authors and Subjects with the categories Persons and Things; hence the hybrid Name Catalogue which consists, usually, of personal author entries and authors as subjects, and needs to be complemented by a second catalogue of authors and subjects which are not personal names.

In spite of all we may do to simplify the subject catalogue, to smooth the path of the enquirer, there will inevitably be some who, through innate lack of confidence or discouraging earlier experiences with indexes, will need to be personally assisted in their approach to the catalogue. Personal assistance may be conceived as either (a) locating the information required, or (b) locating the information required and in the process demonstrating how information is located. The extent to which (b) is attempted in industrial and research libraries will depend upon the conception of the management or parent body as to the role of the library in the larger organisation : it may be economically more efficient for the librarians to carry out searches rather than to try to educate enquirers into the technique of searching. Where this consideration is not applicable, it is desirable that enquirers should not merely be helped but shown how they may help themselves. If library resources are to be fully exploited, it is essential for librarians to see themselves, not only as bibliographical waiters, but as instructors in self service as well. A very little understanding by the enquirer of the librarian's method of work will go a long way towards building up his confidence in the subject catalogue, especially in its ability to lead him to a subject which he has not succeeded in formulating precisely to himself. Such confidence requires as its factual basis an adequate and systematic expression of subject relationship in the catalogue.

### THE SUBJECT CATALOGUE IN REFERENCE SERVICE

The matters so far discussed in this chapter are in the nature of preliminaries; how to present the catalogue to newcomers, how to overcome inhibitions and to avoid misunderstandings as to its use. Assuming that these obstacles are more or less successfully surmounted, we must now consider in a more positive way how the subject catalogue is used for tracing information. It will be convenient to look at the matter from the point of view of the librarian doing reference work and searching for information on behalf of enquirers, but it should be apparent that this viewpoint is not essentially different from that of the intelligent enquirer who is able to search for himself.

The subject catalogue enters into the work of the reference librarian at the point at which his personal knowledge or recollection of the material in the library fails. This may seem, and is, a trite and obvious point: it is, however, rather important that the subject catalogue should be seen in proper perspective against the activity of reference work as a whole, which requires minds both well stocked with bibliographical information and well versed in questions of subject relationship. A busy reference department would be crippled if every subject enquiry had to be routed through the catalogue, if there were no one available with the necessary knowledge of bibliographical short cuts and the accumulated acquaintance with sources derived from constant handling of enquiries. In a small library, particularly a small special library, knowledge by the staff of the books or documents themselves will adequately account for the majority of requests received. But few reference librarians are in this fortunate position: many control stocks, the detailed contents of which are far beyond the capacity of personal memory to recall. The collective enquiry which asks for all available information upon the subject will almost always demand the use of the subject catalogue.

Searching in the subject catalogue is in one sense the subject cataloguing and classifying process in reverse. Ideally the person who handles enquiries involving the subject catalogue should also have been its compiler. This is not usually feasible, but it is desirable that reference library assistants should combine with knowledge of bibliography some understanding of the nature of what has been called subject catalogue language and its underlying basis in term relationship and classification. It is a commonplace that the reference librarian must clearly understand just what the subject is which is being sought. He should also have a fairly explicit idea of its relationship to other subjects in its vicinity in the field of knowledge. The disentangling of the complexities of composite subjects can be undertaken most effectively with the aid of a few mental frames of reference, such as that in Science, a composite subject may include components denoting Object Studied, Material, Phenomena, Method of Study; that in Technology the fundamental categories are Product, Material, Process, and Problems arising out of the Processes; that in the Fine Arts the entities encountered are Artist, Subject depicted, Medium, and Decorative Use; that in the Social sciences, the Group and the Activities connected with it are the constantly recurring ideas. These are of course the 'facets' which lie at the root of the heading language of the subject catalogue. While the catalogue does not demand that the user should know this language, the latter's task is expedited and his searching systematised if the subject of the enquiry is first mentally coded into subject catalogue language. This preliminary exercise also confers upon the reference librarian who may be handling an unfamiliar subject a rapid method of clarifying his appreciation of its relation to more familiar ground. In other words, it assists him to orientate himself.

## SEARCH STRATEGY – THE CLASSIFIED CATALOGUE

Let us now attempt to trace out in detail the route of search for material in a classified catalogue on the *B.N.B.* pattern, and in an alphabetico-specific catalogue with a connective reference system based upon the same classificatory pattern, as outlined in Chapter XI.[1] The route will be the same whether the enquiry is for a piece of specific information or requires the collection of all available information, the only difference being that in the first case it will terminate as soon as the information is found, and in the second it will traverse all the stages which we are about to consider. The essential stages of search are the same in both of the two forms of catalogue under discussion, and they embrace the following : (a) material on the specific subject called for, (b) material on each generic subject in the hierarchy containing the specific subject, beginning with the least general and proceeding hierarchically upwards, (c) collateral subjects collocated in the systematic section of the classified catalogue with the specific subject and the lower of the generic subjects mentioned in (b), (d) collateral subjects collocated with the specific subject or the lower generic subjects, either in the alphabetical subject index to the classified catalogue or in the alphabetico-specific catalogue.

We may now try to apply this strategic framework to the search in a classified catalogue incorporating D.C. arrangement of the systematic section, facet analysis and chain procedure, as outlined in Chapter X. We will assume that a comprehensive search is to be made for all material available in the library on a subject of moderate complexity, namely 'Flame Spectrum analysis to determine trace elements in the Stems of Grasses'.

The first step is to classify the subject of the enquiry, i.e., to arrange the verbal components in an order which would fix the location of the subject in the catalogue if it were represented by a whole document. This rearrangement of verbal components gives us

    Grasses
        Stems
            Chemistry
                Trace elements
                    Determination
                      Analysis
                        Spectrum
                          Flame

The subject is next sought in the subject index, where the order of terms is the reverse of that just given. If the library has a document on the subject we should therefore expect to find in the subject index

    Flame : Spectrum : Determination : Trace elements : Stems : Grasses

this entry would direct to the D.C. symbol 584.9[1], and bearing in mind the classificatory order of components given above, we should have no difficulty in locating in the classified file

    584.9[1] – Stems. Chemistry. Trace elements. Determination. Analysis.
                Spectrum analysis. Flame

if present. Whether the subject is present or otherwise, we proceed to examine in succession

    584.9[1] – Stems. Chemistry. Trace elements. Determination. Analysis.
                Spectrum analysis
    584.9[1] – Stems. Chemistry. Trace elements. Determination. Analysis
    584.9[1] – Stems. Chemistry. Trace elements
    584.9[1] – Stems. Chemistry
    584.9[1] – Stems
    584.9      Grasses
    584        Monocotyledons
    583/584   Angiosperms

| 582 | Seed plants |
| 580 | Botany |
| 574 | Biology |
| 500 | Science |

The whole object of hierarchical arrangement is, of course, to facilitate such a hierarchical search. Needless to say, the catalogue user will not examine every document under the headings given here. The subject is of rather specialised interest, and, from Monocotyledons onwards, the search will obviously confine itself to advanced treatises, encyclopædias, indexes to periodicals and abstracts.

Had there been no entry in the subject index under

Flame : Spectrum : Analysis : Trace elements : Stems : Grasses

it would have been necessary to seek, in the subject index, entries for each of the generic subjects given above.

Spectrum : Analysis : Trace elements : Stems : Grasses
Analysis : Trace elements : Stems : Grasses
Trace elements : Stems : Grasses

and so on hierarchically upwards. As soon as one of these subjects is found in the subject index, the remainder of the hierarchical search is continued within the classified file.

On completion of the hierarchical search, the searcher proceeds to examine headings collateral in the classified file with the earlier members of the hierarchical series. Systematic collateral relationships between subjects are not all of equal closeness or significance for searching purposes. Possibly significant collaterals of our specific subject are :

584.9[1] – Stems. Chemistry. Trace elements. Determination. Analysis. Spectrum analysis. Arc

584.9[1] – Stems. Chemistry. Trace elements. Determination. Analysis. Spectrum analysis. Spark

The likelihood of works entered under these headings containing the required material on flame spectra is not very great, but a routine search should be made. Systematic collaterals of some of the lower generic terms already examined should also be briefly reviewed at this stage. The systematic collaterals of Spectrum determination of Trace elements in Grass Stems are, of course, other analytical techniques, such as chromatography, applied to the same situation. It is just possible that some of these might include significant references to flame spectrographic analysis, but the chances are low, and checking of collateral relatives of terms above this generic level would hold only remote possibilities of bringing in the material required. On the whole, systematic collaterals are not likely to include required information unless the relationship is a very close one. For the classified catalogue it is, however, convenient to make a check of entries under systematic collaterals at this stage, since they are readily accessible in the classified file side by side with each member of the hierarchical series.

The final stage of search, the checking of material under alphabetical collateral headings, requires a return to the subject index. Each concept of the hierarchical series has now to be considered in the context of its immediate neighbours in the subject index. We recall that the specific subject in index form is given as

Flame : Spectrum : Analysis: Trace elements : Stems : Grasses

In the immediate vicinity in the index, we may find such entries as

| | |
|---|---|
| Flame : Spectrum : Biochemistry | 574.19[1] |
| Flame : Spectrum : Clinical pathology | 616.075[1] |
| Flame : Spectrum : Manganese | 546.71[1] |
| Flame : Spectrum : Molecular structure : Physics | 539.1[1] |

With the background obtained during the course of the hierarchical search it should be clear to the searcher that the first two topics indexed above may well contain data germane to the enquiry.

The first generic term appears in the subject index, perhaps in the following context :

| | |
|---|---|
| Spectrum : Analysis : Biochemistry | 574.19[1] |
| Spectrum : Analysis : Clinical pathology | 616.075[1] |
| Spectrum : Analysis : Effluents : Atmospheric pollution | 628.52[1] |
| Spectrum : Analysis : Leaves : Root crops : Soil chemistry | 631.42[1] |
| Spectrum : Analysis : Manganese | 546.71[1] |
| Spectrum : Analysis : Stars | 523.87 |
| Spectrum : Analysis : Stems : Grasses | 584.9[1] |
| Spectrum : Analysis : Vinyl mixtures | 547.22[1] |

The searcher will already, when looking at the entries on Flame spectrum determination of Manganese and Biochemical materials, have glanced at the collocated entries on general spectrum analysis in the same applications, so there will be no point in returning again. to 574.19[1] or 546.71[1] in the classified file. Spectrum analysis of the stars and of effluents is clearly so far from the subject of our enquiry that entries under these headings can be ignored, but the spectrum analysis of the leaves of root crops to determine soil constituents may include relevant material, and the entries on this subject should be examined.

The next generic topic in the subject index

Analysis : Trace elements : Stems : Grasses      584.9[1]

appears in context with a large number of index entries denoting various aspects and applications of analytical chemistry. Among them it is possible that there might be some apposite to the enquiry, such as

Analysis : Grass : Fodder : Livestock      636.0862[1]

and material under this heading should be checked in the classified file.

The next generic entry to be looked up in the index is

Trace elements : Chemistry : Stems : Grasses      584.9[1]

Its neighbours in the index are perhaps

Trace elements : Chemistry : Botany      581.19[1]
Trace elements : Chemistry : Fish      597.[1]
Trace elements : Hydroponics      635.[1]
Trace elements : Vegetables : Dietetics      613.26[1]

The first entry here offers a line worth pursuing, and, while in the classified file we take the opportunity of examining its generic, 581.19 Plant Biochemistry.

The next generic term in the subject index is

Chemistry : Stems : Grasses      584.9[1]

and among a large group of entries under the entry word 'Chemistry' we select the following as likely to justify searching :

Chemistry : Herbaceous plants      582.13[1]
Chemistry : Stems : Cereals      633.1[1]

The next generic entry

Stems : Grasses      584.9[1]

might possibly be accompanied by usefully related subjects in a botanical library. The next generic entry in the subject index

Grasses : Botany      584.9

has as a neighbour

Grasses : Crops : Agriculture      633.2

which would merit following up in the classified file.

It is unlikely that the alphabetical collaterals of the remaining terms in the hierarchical series will include relevant information, and this exhausts what might be termed the formal strategy of search. It is, however, likely that the process of examining literature under the various generic terms will bring to light other subjects related to the sought topic. Such relationships may not be indicated in the catalogue, owing to the fact that no whole document on the subjects concerned is held by the library. Thus, in examining the literature on Trace elements in plant biochemistry, the searcher may have brought to his attention the fact that trace elements are often components of metal enzymes. This relationship, we may assume, is not brought to light because there is no document wholly on metal enzymes. This piece of extra-catalogue information suggests that treatises on enzymes in general might profitably be included in the search. We have here a partial answer to criticisms of the catalogue composed mainly of subject headings covering the subjects of whole documents, as opposed to attempts to codify by mechanical means all subjects mentioned in the documents. If the catalogue is constructed upon the former principle, the relationships which can be shown are obviously limited to those concerning subjects represented by whole documents. Other relationships which would be apparent in the catalogue only if extensive analytical subject cataloguing were practised are often, in fact, encountered in the process of generic search.

### SEARCH STRATEGY – THE ALPHABETICO-SPECIFIC CATALOGUE

The procedure for searching an alphabetical subject catalogue constructed as described in Chapter XI is a fairly close parallel to that carried out in the classified catalogue. In this case the first step is to formulate the enquiry in the language of alphabetical subject headings :

GRASSES, Stems, Trace elements, Flame spectrum analysis

The catalogue structure outlined in Chapter XI included references from specific to generic subjects, except in cases where both subjects were entered under the same entry word. In such cases, the immediate generic subject is obtained, either by removing the last component in the heading 'Flame Spectrum Analysis', or checking to see if the catalogue includes a heading which substitutes a generic term for the last component. Applying this to our example, we may find that the catalogue includes the headings

GRASSES, Stems, Trace elements, Spectrum analysis
GRASSES, Stems, Trace elements, Analysis

These are equivalent to the second and third members of the hierarchical series listed in connection with the search in the classified catalogue, and entries under each are now examined in the alphabetical subject catalogue. We may assume that no further substitution generics are to be found at the same level of subheading, so the next generic subject heading to be searched is

GRASSES, Stems, Trace elements

One substitution generic is to be found at the subheading level of Trace elements; this is

GRASSES, Stems, Chemistry

which is searched accordingly. The next generic heading will be

GRASSES, Stems

Under Grasses there are no other subheadings which could be substitution generics for Stems, so that

GRASSES

may be taken as the next generic heading. From this point upwards-directing 'see also' references indicate to the searcher each generic stage, and each is searched as in the classified catalogue.

The second stage of search in the classified catalogue was concerned with the systematic collateral relatives of each of the concepts which had been encountered in the preceding hierarchical search. The probability of useful information being gathered from these sources was not rated very highly, but it was convenient to carry out this part of the search at the second stage because all the entries on systematic collaterals were ready to hand in the classified file. This consideration has no weight in the alphabetical subject catalogue, where the entries on systematic collateral subjects, though indicated by 'see also' or similar references, are physically separated. They can be left until the more profitable alphabetical collaterals have been searched.

The search of alphabetical collaterals in the alphabetical subject catalogue involves reviewing headings and references which are adjacent to each *verbal component* forming part of the headings looked up in the preceding generic search. These generic headings were :

GRASSES, Stems, Trace elements, Flame spectrum analysis
GRASSES, Stems, Trace elements, Spectrum analysis
GRASSES, Stems, Trace elements, Analysis
GRASSES, Stems, Trace elements, Chemistry

GRASSES, Stems, Trace elements
GRASSES, Stems
GRASSES
MONOCOTYLEDONS
ANGIOSPERMS
SEED PLANTS
BOTANY
BIOLOGY
SCIENCE

Starting at the specific heading and listing components in left-to-right order, and quoting none more than once, we are left with the following places to be consulted for the possible presence of significant alphabetical collaterals :

| GRASS | STEMS | TRACE ELEMENTS |
|---|---|---|
| FLAME SPECTRUM | SPECTRUM | ANALYSIS |
| CHEMISTRY | MONOCOTYLEDONS | ANGIOSPERMS |
| SEED PLANTS | BOTANY | BIOLOGY |
| SCIENCE | | |

Possibly useful collateral headings which may be found in certain of these positions are as follows :

{ GRASSES, Agriculture
{ GRASS, Fodder, Analysis

STEMS, Cereals, Chemistry   *See* CEREALS, Stems, Chemistry

TRACE ELEMENTS, Plants   *See* PLANTS, Trace elements

{ FLAME SPECTRA, Biochemistry
{ FLAME SPECTRA, Manganese   *See* MANGANESE, Flame spectra

SPECTRUM ANALYSIS, Root crops, Soil chemistry   *See* ROOT CROPS, Spectrum analysis, Soil chemistry

CHEMISTRY, Herbaceous plants   *See* HERBACEOUS PLANTS, Chemistry

In these examples of alphabetical collateral subjects we have covered exactly the same ground as in the alphabetical collateral search in the subject index of the classified catalogue, though there is some variation in the order of search reflecting differences between component order in alphabetico-specific catalogue headings on the one hand and chain procedure entries in the subject index of the classified catalogue on the other.

There remains the search of entries under systematic collateral headings. These are indicated either by references, or if collateral references are omitted as a matter of policy, they may be discovered by a two stage-approach via an upwards-reference to a generic heading and then a downwards-reference to all the topics contained in the generic heading. If direct collateral references are omitted, the two stage procedure calls for greater discrimination on the part of the searcher in deciding which collaterals are likely to yield useful information.

The search routine outlined in this chapter is in some ways a complementary aspect of the fact that the subject catalogue under discussion is based upon headings which, in the main, refer to the contents of whole documents. If a smaller indexing unit were chosen, search procedure would be rather simpler. It would be very much simpler if the subject catalogue were a vast amalgamation of the indexes of every document in the library. It would consist only of a hierarchical search. Such a conception of a subject catalogue as a record of every detail of the thought content of documents underlies the thinking of some workers[2] in machine retrieval who contemplate coding whole abstracts into machine-index language. Such a catalogue is likely to be useful in inverse proportion to the width of the subject field of the library concerned. Where the stock includes treatises it would be repetitious, as a high proportion of terms indexed in works on the same subject are common to all the works concerned. In this latter case the solution of the problem of information retrieval would seem to lie in subject summarisation at the level of the whole document, coupled with an organised search strategy.

## ANALYTICAL SUBJECT ENTRIES AND SEARCH PROCEDURE

It was mentioned above that in so far as headings refer to whole documents alone, the only subject relationships which can be expressed in the catalogue are those which comprehend subjects represented by whole documents. This is not quite true for chain procedure, as this provides access from appropriate generic headings which may possess no corresponding documents. Thus we may have books on Sound Radio, Telephony and Television, but no volume on Electrical Communication in general. Under chain procedure we nevertheless subject index under Electrical Communication, provided that any part of this subject is represented by a document in the library. But we have no similar automatic 'array procedure' whereby, for instance, whenever we have a book on Electricity, we refer to it from its collateral Magnetism, irrespective of there already being documents on the latter in the library. It is perhaps also worth noting that the systematically constructed catalogue cannot show the kind of relationships characterised in the description of Library of Congress practice in Chapter VII as 'false collaterals' (e.g., that between Classicism and Aesthetics) until a book is catalogued dealing with both topics as components in a composite subject (e.g., Aesthetics of Classicism).

Analytical subject entries represent departures from the indexing unit of one summary heading per document. They are used for documents which are devoted to more than one subject or to a single concept which cannot be expressed as a unitary idea. Analytical subject entries are made from parts of documents which will be missed by a search strategy which relies upon whole document headings plus indication of hierarchical relationships. Thus if a book is given a subject heading corresponding to its overall subject, no analytical entries will be needed for parts of the book on divisions of the subject, so scheduled in the underlying classification scheme of either classified or alphabetico-specific catalogue. Thus if the author's concept of the scope of his subject is wider than that implied in the classification scheme, an analytical subject entry will enable the marginal to be recovered in the course of searching. There is some justification for restricting analytical entry for bi-topical books in which the two subjects are topics collaterals in the classification. Since collateral searching is routine, it would be possible to omit the subsidiary entry for the minor subject, provided that its presence is made clear in the title or annotation of the main subject entry, and also provided that the catalogue already includes some material on the minor subject.

Multi-topical books containing several subjects which fall within a particular generic class demand a decision as to whether they shall be given class entry or multiple entry under the separate topics. If the number of the latter is less than the permissible economic limit of subject headings allowed per book, and if they together comprise less, let us say, than two-thirds of the field covered by the class heading, then multiple entry is a better policy. If placed at the class heading, the entry would be redundant for one-third of all searches (assuming all parts of the subject to be in equal demand), and as such would constitute a gratuitous hindrance, comparable to the false drops of a mechanical retrieval system. The entry can, of course, be placed out of harm's way from the point of view of most specific searches by being given some such subheading as 'Non-comprehensive works' ; but it would not thereby escape inclusion in collective searches.

## NOTES AND REFERENCES

[1] See also Coates, E. J. *Classification in reference service*. Annals of Libr. Sc., Vol. 1, 1954, pp. 151–161, and Foskett, D. J. *Catalogues and reference service.* Librarian, Vol. 41, No. 11, 1952, pp. 213–218.

[2] As for instance, Perry, J. W., Kent, A. and Berry, M. M. in their *Machine literature searching* (Cleveland (Ohio), 1956), pp. 100–108.

CHAPTER XIV

# THE ROLE OF CONVENTIONAL CLASSIFICATION
## SCHEMES

THIS book has attempted to deal with some of the problems which arise when an attempt is made to build subject catalogues, classified or alphabetical, upon a systematic basis of some kind. No claim is made to have foreseen every difficulty which will arise, and even among the matters discussed there are several which have been only partially clarified. But it is hoped that enough has been said to persuade those who may be planning subject catalogues that there is an alternative to the extremes on the one hand of blind dependence upon standard lists, which are purely retrospective in conception and offer no solutions to the problem of developing subjects, and on the other of following the variable promptings of personal intuition and hoping that the final result will not have omitted too many essentials.

One query may remain in the minds of readers which will possibly cause them to doubt the wisdom of trying to apply practically the principles which have been discussed. Repeatedly in earlier chapters reference has been made to the shortcomings of the classification schemes in general use. Specific subjects are too often placed under wrong generic terms, modulation of hierarchical chains is not fully carried out, makeshifts are resorted to in order to present an appearance of solving problems of subject interpolation which are insoluble, given the determination to preserve old rigid notations inviolate; breakdown of subjects by superficial characteristics is perpetuated in successive revisions. Gross errors in classification schemes require, where possible, to be sidestepped by the cataloguer if they are not to find fresh expression in the subject catalogue, and pervasive faults in the classification scheme result in a certain clumsiness in the manner in which subject relationship is expressed in the subject catalogue. In view of these deficiencies, it may be asked, would it not be better to await the arrival of a more effective classification scheme[1] towards which some research efforts are now being directed? Is it not a mistake to expend effort in building upon foundations which are manifestly inadequate?

There are two answers to this. In the first place, the practical need is an urgent one. Information is now of unprecedented importance in human affairs, yet the foundationless subject catalogue returns desultory answers when we try to use it for the recovery of information. What seem to the writer somewhat disproportionate hopes now centred upon mechanical information retrieval appear to reflect disillusionment and lack of confidence in the manually-operated subject catalogue. Machine retrievers of information are themselves confronted by similar problems of logical structure, which their inventions have made more urgent. The machine, no less than its manual counterpart, needs a logical programme in order to be effectively utilised.

The second reason why practical experiment in systematically-based subject cataloguing should not wait for future developments in classification, is that it may well help to speed up those developments. Anomalies in chain procedure subject entries are often referable to structural errors previously unnoticed in the classification schedule. Further study is needed at the practical level, of compound subject terms, the relationships between components, and the relative significance of the components, possibly including the ways in which this may be indicated in the spoken language by stress and intonation. It is to be expected that advances in understanding of the factors involved in subject naming, in the processes of terminological development, may throw light upon still obscure questions in subject classification. The fact that the meanings of words are often ambiguous, and not to be taken at their face value, should not cause us to ignore the connection, fragmentary and tortuous though it be, between linguistic pre-logic and the logical problems which confront us in classification. Research in classification is making an attempt to forge an instrument of communication without the crudities of natural language; but we should not overlook the fact that natural language is the soil out of which classification has grown. In the future development of classification it would be most unwise to disregard the hints and intimations which ordinary language offers on concept relationships. Neither in its theory nor in its practice can classification detach itself completely from its affiliations with language. It is this middle country between classification and natural language which has been reconnoitred in this book.

## NOTES AND REFERENCES

[1] See Classification Research Group. *The need for a faceted classification as the basis of all methods of information retrieval.* Libr. Assoc. Record, Vol. 57, 1955, pp. 262–268.

# INDEX

Material–Thing relationship, Table opp.
p. 55
Matter (Ranganathan), 44
Mechanical selector, 11, 12, 14, 15, 172,
175
and indexing unit, 15, 171
Memory, personal, and catalogue defici-
encies, 18
Metcalfe, J., 98n, 128, 134n, 149, 159
Miller, G. R., 46
Mills, J., 134n
Minute topics v. locality, 62
Modulation, classificatory terms, 113
Colon Classification, 113, 114
Decimal Classification, 118, 131
reflected in chain procedure, 89
Modulation, feature headings, 122
Multidimensional relationships, alpha-
betical subject catalogues, 70, 71
Multiple entry, classified catalogue, 16
Multi-topical documents, 16, 172

Name Catalogue, 161
Natural language, 11, 175
component order
modified by significance order, 52
phrase headings, 21
forms, Cutter, 60
Kaiser system, 41
relationships expressed in 52, 55, 64n,
147
Neutral subject catalogue, 17, 48
defined, 12
New subjects, 32
Non-specific subject entry, and collateral
references, 147
Notation, classification, 10, 16
non-hierarchical
British Catalogue of Music Classifi-
cation, 132
Decimal Classification, 116, 117
Notation, relational, 47, 48
Noun
in adjective–noun phrases, 35
replacing adjective, chain procedure,
89
Noun–noun phrases, 22, 23
B.N.B. practice, 126
Noun–preposition–noun phrases. *See*
Prepositional phrases
Noun v. adjective form of place name, 62

'Of' as relation indicator, 52, 53, Table
opp. p. 55
'made of', 53

'Operated by' as relation indicator,
Table opp. p. 55
Operation, method of, v. ultimate func-
tion, 54
Operator, 47, 48, 100

Palmer, B. I., 13n, 49n
Panoramic character, classed cat., 159
Part, 54, 57
designating Kind, 55, 57
Part–Thing relationship, 53, Table opp.
p. 55, 57
Period v. locality, 63
Permutation
classification symbols, classified file,
90, 91, 93, 95–7
terms, 106
classified catalogue subj. index., 88
B.N.B, 130
British Catalogue of Music, 134
chain procedure, 119
Farradane system, 48
Perry, J. W., 173n
Personal assistance to enquirers, 161
Personal knowledge of library material,
reference service, 162
Personality (Ranganathan), 44, 45
Pettee, J., *Subject headings: history and
theory*, 9, 13n, 38n, 43, 66, 69, 70,
79n, 82, 98n
Philosophical topics v. locality, 61, 62
Library of Congress, 77
Phrases, 21, 22, 23
Adjective–noun, 22, 24, 35, 40
as subheadings, 74, 138
B.N.B. subject index, 126, 127, 130
dictionary catalogue, 31, 32, 34, 35
inverted, 21, 35
arrangement, 78
as subheadings, 74, 125, 126
ethnic adjectives, 77
library of Congress headings, 75, 77
noun–noun, 22, 23, 126
Prepositional, 22, 23, 52, 53, 54, 55,
Table opp. p. 55, 56, 58
v. subheadings, 23, 24, 58–9
B.N.B subject index, 126, 127
Place-names. *See* Locality
Plural form of heading, 23, 24, 59, 60
Plural interpretation, caused by lack of
relational words, 127, 128
Political v. geographical names, 77
Pollard, A. F., 30n
Preferred deductive order, 49